Step-By-Step Optimization

With

Excel Solver

The Excel Statistical Master
(that'll be you!)

By Mark Harmon

mark@ExcelMasterSeries.com
www.ExcelMasterSeries.com
ISBN: 978-1-937159-15-3

Reader Testimonials

"I do strategic planning for large enterprise IT projects. While I was familiar with Excel Solver from my MBA class, this book opened a world of ideas to me. The examples are fantastic and gave me great ideas into how set up my problems into solver.

For me, the best part of the book is the insight it provides into reading and translating the reports that solver generates. When I am presenting my solutions to senior management and I am asked what if something changed, I can very quickly answer based on a sensitivity analysis and my interpretation of the report.

Overall a great book that is very easy to read, understand and implement. Thanks Mr. Harmon, keep up the good work."

Michael Langebeck
Morrisville, North Carolina

"I'm finished with school (Financial Economics major) and currently work for a fortune 400 company as a business analyst. I find that the statistics and optimization manuals are indispensable reference tools throughout the day.

I keep both eManuals loaded on my ipad at all times just in case I have to recall a concept I don't use all the time. Its easier to recall the concepts from the eManuals rather then trying to sift through the convoluted banter in a text book, and for that I applaud the author!

In a business world where I need on demand answers now this optimization eManual is the perfect tool.

I just recently used the bond investment optimization problem to build a model in excel and help my VP understand that a certain process we're doing wasn't maximizing our resources.

That's the great thing about this manual, you can use any practice problem (with a little outside thinking) to mold it into your own real life problem and come up with answers that matter in the work place!!"

Sean Ralston
Sr. Financial Analyst
Enogex LLC
Oklahoma City, Oklahoma

"Step-By-Step Optimization With Excel Solver is the "Missing Manual" for the Excel Solver. It is pretty difficult to find good documentation anywhere on solving optimization problems with the Excel Solver. This book came through like a champ!

Optimization with the Solver is definitely not intuitive, but this book is. I found it very easy to work through every single one of the examples. The screen shots are clear and the steps are presented logically. The downloadable Excel spreadsheet with all example completed was quite helpful as well.

Once again, it really amazing how little understandable documentation there is on doing real-life optimization problems with Solver.

For example, just try to find anything anywhere about the well-known Traveling Salesman Problem (a salesman needs to find the shortest route to visit all customers once). It is a tricky problem for sure, but this book showed a quick and easy way to get it done. I'm not sure I would have ever figured that problem out, or some the other problems in the book, without this manual.

I can say that this is the book for anyone who wants or needs to get up to speed on an advanced level quickly with the Excel Solver. It appears that every single aspect of using the Solver seems to be covered thoroughly and yet simply. The author presents a lot of tricks in how to set the correct Solver settings to get it to do exactly what you want.

The book flows logically. It's an easy read. Step-By-Step Optimization With Excel Solver got me up to speed on the Solver quickly and without to much mental strain at all. I can definitely recommend this book."

Pam Copus
Sonic Media Inc.

"As Graduate student of the Graduate Program in International Studies (GPIS) at Old Dominium University, I'm required to have a thorough knowledge of Excel in order to use it as a tool for interpreting data, conducting research and analysis.

I've always found the Excel Solver to be one of the more difficult Excel tools to totally master. Not any more. This book was so clearly written that I was able to do almost every one of advanced optimization examples in the book as soon as I read through it once.

I can tell that the author really made an effort to make this manual as intuitive as possible. The screen shots were totally clear and logically presented.

Some of the examples that were very advanced, such as the venture capital investment example, had screen shot after screen shot to ensure clarity of the difficult Excel spreadsheet and Solver dialogue boxes.

It definitely was "Step-By-Step" just like the title says. I must say that I did have to cheat a little bit and look at the Excel spreadsheet with all of the book's example that is downloadable from the book. The spreadsheet was also a great help.

Step-By-Step Optimization With Excel Solver is not only totally easy to understand and follow, but it is also very complete. I feel like I'm a master of the Solver. I have purchased a couple of other books in the Excel MaSter Series (the Excel Statistical Master and the Advanced Regression in Excel book) and they have all been excellent.

I am lucky to have come across this book because the graduate program that I am in has a number of optimization assignments using the Solver. Thanks Mark for such an easy-to-follow and complete book on using the Solver. It really saved me a lot of time in figuring this stuff out."

Federico Catapano
Graduate Student
International Studies Major
Old Dominion University
Norfolk, Virginia

"Excel Solver is a tool that most folks never use. I was one of those people. I was working on a project, and was told that solver might be helpful. I did some research online, and was more confused than ever. I started looking for a book that might help me. I got this book, and was not sure what to expect.

It surpassed my expectations! The book explains the concepts behind the solver, the best way to set up the "problem", and how to use the tool effectively. It also gives many examples including the files. The files are stored online, and you can download them so you can see everything in excel.

The author does a fantastic job on this book. While I'm not a solver "expert", I am definitely much smarter about it than I was before. Trust me, if you need to understand the solver tool, this book will get you there! "

Scott Kinsey
Missouri

"The author, Mark, has a writing style that is easy to follow, simple, understandable, with clear examples that are easy to follow. This book is no exception.

Mark explains how solver works, the different types of solutions that can be obtained and when to use one or another, explains the content and meaning of the reports available. Then he presents several examples, goes about defining each problem, setting it up in excel and in solver and interpreting the solution.

It is a really good book that teaches you how to apply solver (linear programming) to a problem.

Luis R. Heimpel
El Paso, Texas

Table of Contents

Table of Contents 7

Excel Solver Overview..12

Installing the Excel Solver 14

Optimization Basics With Excel Solver 22

Always Start By Diagramming the Model On Paper 23

Make the Model As Simple and Intuitive As Possible............ 23

Step 1 – Determine the Objective 23

Step 2 – Determine the Decision Variables............................ 24

Step 3 – Build the Excel Equations That Combine the Objective With All Decision Variables 24

Step 4 – List all Constraints... 26

Step 5 – Test the Excel Spreadsheet 27

Step 6 – Insert All Data into the Solver Dialogue Box............ 28

1) The Objective Cell... 29

2) Minimize or Maximize the Target 29

3) Decision Variables... 29

4) Constraints 29

Make Unconstrained Variables Non-Negative 30

Integer Constraints... 30

Binary Constraints 30

Alldifferent Constraints 31

5) Solving Method 31

Simplex LP Method 32

GRG Nonlinear Method 32

Evolutionary Method 34

A Solver Solution's 3 Possible Degrees of Optimality 35

Globally Optimal 35

Locally Optimal 35

Good 35

Convex and Non-Convex Functions 36

Solver Option Settings 37

All Methods – Option Settings 37

GRG Nonlinear Option Settings 40

Evolutionary Option Settings 43

Interpreting Solver Results Messages 46

Messages When Solver Encounters a Problem While Solving
.... 46

Solver could not find a feasible solution 46

The problem is too large for Solver to handle 47

The Objective Cell values do not converge 47

The linearity conditions required by this LP Solver are not satisfied 48

Solver encountered an error value in the objective cell or a constraint cell 48

There is not enough memory available to solve the problem.......... 49

Messages When Solver Found a Problem With Constraints 50

All variables must have both upper and lower bounds 50

Variable bounds conflict in binary or alldifferent constraint.......... 50

Lower and upper bounds on variables allow no feasible solution... 50

Messages When Solver Finds a Solution.................................. 51

Solver found a solution. All constraints and optimality conditions are satisfied.. 51

Solver has converged to the current solution. All constraints are satisfied... 51

Solver cannot improve the current solution. All constraints are satisfied... 52

Solver found an integer solution within tolerance. All constraints are satisfied...53

Solver converged in probability to a global solution 53

Messages When ESC Is Pressed or a Solving Limit Is Reached... 54

Solver stopped at user's request.. 54

Stop chosen when the maximum time limit was reached 54

Stop chosen when the maximum iteration limit was reached......... 54

Stop chosen when the maximum number of [integer] subproblems was reached 54

Understanding Solver Reports.. 56

Reports Made Available When the Solver Finds a Solution 58

The Answer Report and How To Read It....................................... 58

The Population Report and How To Read It 64

The Limits Report and How To Read It... 67

The Sensitivity Report and How To Read It 69

Reports Made Available In Certain Situations When a Problem Occurs During a Solver Run....................................... 72

The Linearity Report and How To Read It 72

The Feasibility Report and How To Read It 77

Feasibility Bounds Report... 81

Knapsack Example - Optimizing the Loading of a Limited Compartment.. 82

Cutting Stock Example - Optimizing the Cutting of Strips of Sheet to Minimize Waste 92

Machine Selection Example - Selecting Machines to Optimally Fulfill an Order 105

Maximizing Employee Satisfaction Example - Optimal Assignment of Company Assets Among Employees For Maximum Satisfaction.. 115

Shipping Cost Minimization Example - Minimizing the Total Cost of Shipping From Multiple Points To Multiple Points............................127

Outbound Marketing Budget Optimization - Reaching a Required Number of Prospects As Cheaply As Possible With Outbound Marketing 140

Inbound Marketing Budget Optimization - Generating a Required Number of Qualified Leads As Cheaply As Possible With Inbound Marketing...150

Bond Portfolio Optimization Example - Optimizing the Allocation of Bonds in a Portfolio To Maximize Return..158

Optimal Investment Selection Example - Maximizing Investment Return Through Optimal Investment Selection.....................................168

Supplier Shipping/Purchasing Cost Minimization - Minimizing the Total Cost of Purchasing and Shipping From Multiple Suppliers...186

Traveling Salesman Problem - Using the All Different Constraint and the Evolutionary Method To Find the Shortest Path To All Customers 200

How To Perform Nonlinear Regression and Curve Fitting – Using the GRG Nonlinear Method 215

Meet Mark the Author..230

Check Out the Latest Manual in the Excel Master Series.........231

To Download the Excel Workbook Containing All Examples In This Manual 247

Excel Solver Overview

The Excel Solver is a fantastic tool. It is perhaps the most widely used optimization and curve fitting software in the world. The calculations that the Excel Solver performs are complex but the user interface is simple enough that almost anyone can quickly master it.

The science of optimization has grown in stature tremendously over the last decade. So much so that optimization is now a required area of study in many graduate degree programs. The business world has become also become a huge proponent and driver behind the growth of optimization. It is not uncommon for companies to quickly realize savings in the millions of dollars after employing optimization tools such as the Excel Solver to better allocate their limited resources.

The Solver's inclusion in Microsoft Excel makes it the most convenient tool to master optimization. Excel has long ago become the standard in spreadsheet software. Nearly every businessperson has access to and familiarity with Excel. The widespread Microsoft Excel with its built-in Excel Solver provides the perfect platform for anyone to master optimization.

Optimization can be described as maximizing or minimizing a model's single output variable by correctly adjusting the model's input variables. That's exactly what the Excel Solver does. The Excel Solver calculates the values of an Excel model's input variables that will maximize or minimize the value of that Excel model's single output variable.

The Excel model's single output variable to be minimized or maximized is called the Objective. The model's input variables that the Solver will adjust are called the Decision Variables. The Excel Solver only task is to calculate the set of values for all of Excel model's input variables that will result in a minimum or maximum value of its output variable.

Problems solved using the Excel Solver normally must have conditions placed on variables within the Excel model so that the outcome will make sense. An example of an applied condition would be to specify that a production machine cannot produce a negative number of output pieces. Conditions like these applied to an Excel Solver problem are called Constraints.

The correct use of the Excel Solver relies upon knowledge of the proper Solver inputs, the numerous settings of the Excel Solver, the ability to understand the Solver's output reports, and the ability to correctly set up a model in Excel. This manual will provide this practical knowledge to you by running through and completely solving a wide variety of the most well known optimization problems. All aspects of solving each problem will be discussed in simple but complete detail.

After completing this manual, you will find the Excel Solver to be an extremely useful and user-friendly optimization tool.

Installing the Excel Solver

Installing the Solver in Excel 2010 is fairly straight-forward and relatively painless. The Solver ships with (is part of) Excel 2010 as an Add-In that must be activated before it can be used.

The process of activating this Add-In takes about 15 seconds. In summary, simply bring the list of Excel Add-Ins, select the Solver Add-In, hit OK and the Solver will be immediately available for use under the Data tab. We will show all of the Solver installation steps in much more detail.

Let's quickly walk through the Solver installation for Excel 2010 over the next several pages:

First, click the File drop-down menu. On this menu, select Options near the bottom of the menu:

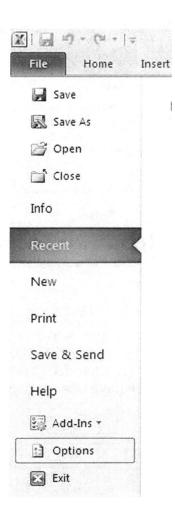

Selecting Options will bring up the following Excel Options menu:

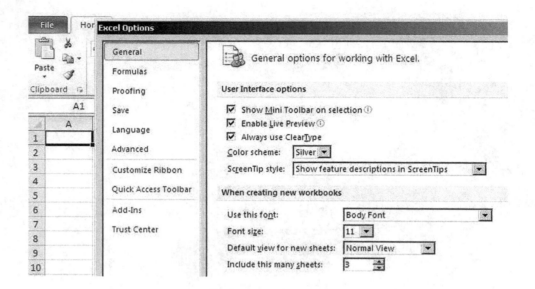

On the Excel Options menu, select Add-Ins near the bottom of this menu. Doing so will bring up the list of available Add-Ins. The Add-ins that appear in this list are all included in Excel 2010 but they are available for use only after they have been activated.

The following menu shows 2 lists of Add-Ins: the upper list of Active Application Add-Ins and the lower list of Inactive Application Add-Ins.

The highlighted Solver Add-In appears in the lower Inactive list and therefore has not yet been activated. As soon as it is activated, the Solver Add-In will then be moved to the upper Active Applications Add-Ins list.

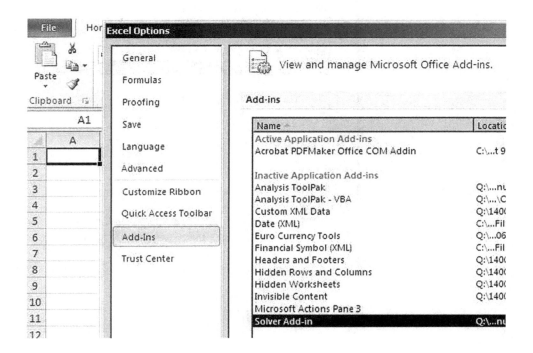

To activate the Solver Add-In, scroll to the bottom of this menu and select Excel Add-Ins from the Manage menu and hit Go as follows:

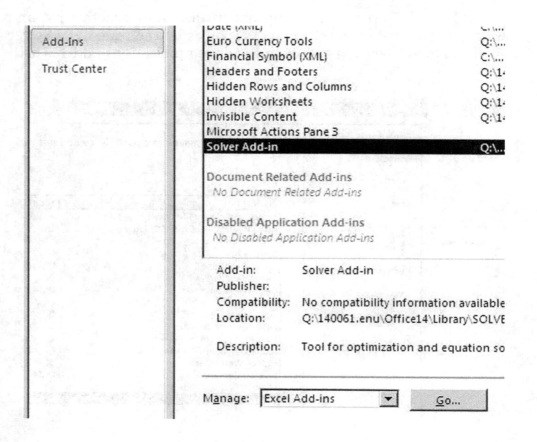

After selecting Excel Add-Ins and hitting Go, the following list of Excel Add-Ins will appear. To activate any of these Add-Ins, simply check the box next to the Add-In you want to activate and then hit OK.

In addition to activating the Solver Add-In, I recommend activating the Analysis ToolPak Add-In as has been done in the following Add-Ins dialogue box. The Analysis ToolPak contains some of Excel's most useful statistical analysis tools such as regression, ANOVA, t-testing, and descriptive statistics.

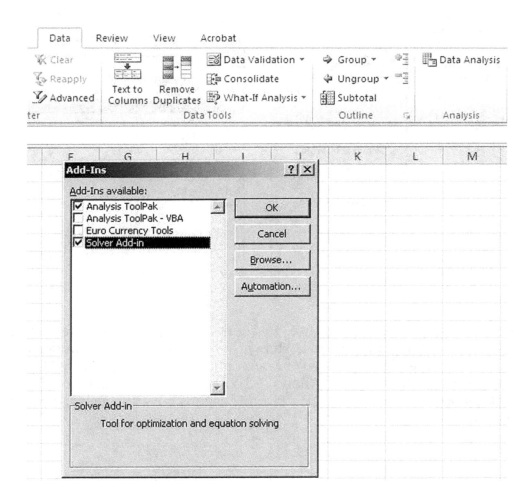

After you have selected Solver Add-In and the Analysis ToolPak and then hit OK, these 2 Add-Ins are now listed in the upper Active Application Add-Ins list as shown next in the following Add-Ins list:

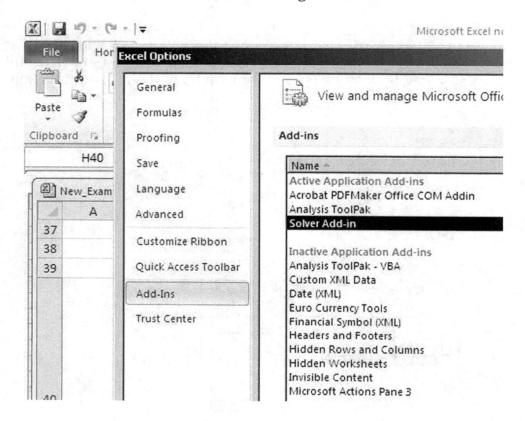

The Solver is available for use as soon as it appears in the Active Application Add-Ins list as it is shown here. You will find it under the Data tab on the right side of your screen as shown next. You will also notice the newly-activated Analysis ToolPak is now available in the Analysis section under the Data tab and right above the Solver link as follows:

Optimization Basics With Excel Solver

To begin working with the Excel Solver, you need first define a mathematical relationship between one or more input variables and a single output variable. The input variable(s) are quantities that you have the ability to change and whose changes will affect the single output variable. These input variables are called **Decision Variables**. The output variable is called the **Objective**.

The Excel Solver calculates the values of all Decision Variables that will maximize or minimize the Objective or cause the Objective to be set to a specific value. ***The Solver only changes the values of Decision Variables during its calculations.*** Any other variables not directly affected by the Decision Variables will not change. These can be replaced with constant values.

Most problems solved with the Excel Solver have **Constraints**. Constraints are conditions or limitations that are imposed on any of the variables that are any part of the equations that calculate the objective.

Always Start By Diagramming the Model On Paper

Always start by diagramming your model on paper. Never start by building your model in Excel. The best preparation for solving any problem with the Excel Solver is to diagram all of your basic equations on paper.

Make the Model As Simple and Intuitive As Possible

If you are new the Excel Solver and are learning it for the first time, opt for simplicity in your model. Set a goal to make your model is as intuitive as possible. Try to set up your model so that any other user could immediately understand the path to the Objective and how each Decision Variable fits into the path.

If possible, try to keep the **Clear Mathematical Path to the Objective** separated from the Constraints. This is not always possible or the most efficient way to solve problems with the Excel Solver but in most cases it will make your model more intuitive to anyone who views your Excel model for the first time. The examples in this book attempt to separate the mathematical path to the Objective from the Constraints. It is not always practical to do this but it has been done in the examples that it can be done efficiently.

Step 1 – Determine the Objective

Determine exactly what the **Objective** is. The Objective is the object to be minimized or maximized. There can be only 1 Objective in a problem. In the Excel model, the Objective's value will be contained in the **Objective Cell** in the Excel spreadsheet. The complete set of equations that are used to calculate the Objective is often referred to in this manual as the **Clear Mathematical Path to the Objective**.

Step 2 – Determine the Decision Variables

After determining the Objective, figure out which variables will control the value of the Objective. These are the set of Decision Variables. All Decision Variables must be directly controllable be you.

The Decision Variables should be the only unknown quantities in the Clear Mathematical Path to the Objective. The Decision Variables are the only things that Solver will change during its calculations. Variables in the model that the Decision Variables do not affect should be set to constants. The Solver will only adjust the values of Decision Variables so any model variables not affected by the Decision Variables will remain unchanged.

Step 3 – Build the Excel Equations That Combine the Objective With All Decision Variables

After you have determined what the Objective and the Decision Variables are, diagram how the Objective will be calculated. This is quite often the trickiest and most important part of Solver optimization. You don't want to put equations on an Excel spreadsheet until you have created on paper a Clear Mathematical Path to the Objective which includes all of the Decision Variables.

One tip when entering a large number of Decision Variables (Changing Variable Cells) in Excel – If you would like to see all of the Decision Variables in the "By Changing Variable Cells" box, you may consider placing the Decision Variables into 1 contiguous block in the Excel model so that you can simply list the upper left and lower right corners of the block to cover them all and not have to list each cell individually.

Explicitly State All Assumptions and Methods Prominently On the Spreadsheet

This is standard practice for anyone who builds Excel models.

Become Familiar With and Use Excel's Auditing Tools

These tools, such as the Trace Precedents tool, are extremely useful when building and troubleshooting Excel models. They can be found in Excel 2010 under the Formulas tab and then click on the Formula Auditing dropdown arrow.

Try Not To Use Constants Inside the Model

A good practice is to place any constants in separate cells outside of the model and then link to those cells from within the model whenever those constants are needed in calculations. If the constant must ever be changed, you can simply change 1 cell. You spreadsheet will also be more intuitive if constants are kept separate and labeled.

Defining Names of Cells Ranges

Another tip that can improve the readability of your Excel model is to name ranges of cells. To name a range of cells in Excel 2010, highlight all of those cells simultaneously and click on the Formulas tab. Select the Define Name option and type in the name you want for that range of cells.

To place this named cell range into the Excel Solver dialogue box, select the named range of cells before opening the Solver dialogue box. Select the named cell range by clicking on the Home tab and then the dropdown arrow in the address bar above the upper left corner of the Excel spreadsheet. A list of all named ranges that you have created will appear. Click on the 1 you want and its cells will be highlighted on the spreadsheet. You can now open up the Solver dialogue box and insert that range as a Constraint, a block of Variable Cells, or an Objective (if the named and highlighted block is just a single cell).

Makes Sure All Excel Inputs Are Scaled Properly

This is an extremely important rule. All inputs should use the same or similar scale if possible. **The values of the Objective, Decision Variables, and Constraints should not be more than a few orders of magnitude different from each other.** Improperly scaled inputs can trigger a number of Solver error messages and stopping conditions.

Step 4 – List All Constraints

After you have created a Clear Mathematical Path to the Objective that includes all Decision Variables, determine what variables in the mathematical path need to have conditions or limitations imposed upon them for the problem to make sense. An example of this would be to specify that a production machine cannot produce a negative number of units. These conditions or limitations are called Constraints.

One tip is to circle any variables in the mathematical path that must be limited or have conditions applied to them. This exercise will expedite setting Constraints in the Excel Solver after you have laid out the equations in the Excel spreadsheet.

Once you have created the Clear Mathematical Path to the Objective and determined what needs to be constrained, you are ready to begin building your model in Excel.

Go ahead and start creating your model in Excel. Excel 2010 is used for all of the examples in this manual. If you are using Excel 2003, you will have to download a free conversion pack from Microsoft that will enable you to open the Excel 2010 or 2007 spreadsheets in Excel 2003. As soon as you attempt to open an Excel 2007 or 2010 workbook (any Excel workbook that uses the ribbon navigation structure instead of drop-down menus), you will be provided a link to download this conversion pack from Microsoft. It is about 35MB in size.

The first Excel step is to construct the Clear Mathematical Path to the Objective in the spreadsheet. When inputting your equations into Excel, **highlight the cells containing the Objective and Decision Variables with unique background colors to make them easy to spot**.

In each Excel model in this manual, all cells containing Decision Variables have been given dark gray backgrounds, all cells containing Constraints have been given medium gray backgrounds, and the cell containing the Objective has been given a light gray background.

It also a good idea to label each Objective cell, Constraint cell, and Decision Variable cell to indicate clearly what it is. The Objective cell, all Constraint cells, and all Decision Variable cells are labeled in all Excel models in this manual.

To improve the efficient of the Excel Solver, always place realistic upper and lower bounds on all variables by using Constraints. This is especially true if you are using the Evolutionary method or the GRG Nonlinear method with the Multistart option.

Step 5 – Test the Excel Spreadsheet

Before you begin to input Constraints into the Excel Solver dialogue box, run the Excel model through its paces to make sure that it correctly calculates the Objective using every different combination of Decision Variables that is appropriate for your problem type. This exercise may point out new Constraints that must be imposed which you had not originally thought of.

Step 6 – Insert All Data into the Solver Dialogue Box

After you have thoroughly and successfully tested your Excel model, you are ready to begin inserting all data into the Solver dialogue box.

Bring up the Excel Solver and the following blank Solver dialogue box comes up:

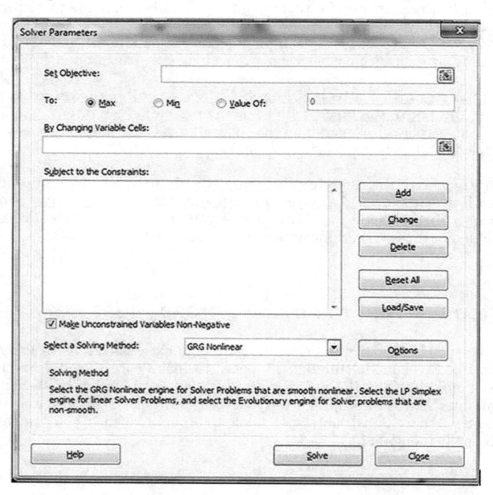

The Solver dialogue box has the following 5 parameters that need to be set:

1) The Objective Cell – This is the target cell in the Excel spreadsheet that you are either trying to maximize, minimize, or set to a certain value.

2) Minimize or Maximize the Target, or attempt to achieve a certain value in the Objective cell.

3) Decision Variables – A set of variables that will be changed by the Excel Solver in order to optimize the target cell.

4) Constraints – These are the limitations that the problem subjects the Solver to during its calculations.

When you are confident that your mathematical path to the Objective produces a correct result using every appropriate combination of Decision Variables, determine which variables in the Excel model must have conditions or limitations imposed upon them. These conditions and limitations are called **Constraints**.

One very important tip when creating Constraints - **Always ensure that Constraints have formulas on the left side and constant numbers or cell containing constant values on the right side**.

The obvious Constraints will be those variables that must be made greater to, less than, or equal to specific values. Less obvious are those variables that cannot be allowed to assume negative values.

Here the settings used to apply the Excel Solver's built-in Constraints:

Make Unconstrained Variables Non-Negative

For example, a production machine could not produce a negative number of items. These variables must have their values limited to being greater or equal to zero. If no variables in the model could be allowed to assume negative values, you can take a short cut and check "Make Unconstrained Variables Non-Negative" instead of individually Constraining each to assume values greater or equal to zero.

Integer Constraints

Some variables in the Clear Mathematical Path to the Objective may have to be limited to assuming whole number (integer) values. The cells in the spreadsheet containing these variables will be set to the Constraint setting "int" which is short for the Solver **Integer Constraint**.

Binary Constraints

Some variables in the Clear Mathematical Path to the Objective may have to be limited to assuming binary (1 or 0) values. These variables usually designate "use or don't use" or "on or off" conditions of other variables in the mathematical path. The cells in the spreadsheet holding these variables will be set to the Constraint setting "bin" which is short for the Solver **Binary Constraint**. The Investment Selection example in this manual applies the Binary Constraint to the Decision Variables which determine whether or not an investment will be made in a particular year.

Alldifferent Constraints

Sometime all of the variables within a group of variables must have different values. All of the cells as a group will be simultaneously set to the Constraint setting "dif," which is short for the Solver **Alldifferent Constraint**. An example of this is shown in the Traveling Salesman Problem in this manual.

Employing any of Solver's built-in Integer Constraints (Integer, Binary, or All Different) can often greatly increase the time that the Excel Solver takes to find a solution.

5) Solving Method - You must choose 1 of the 3 available solving methods. The 3 solving methods are the Simplex LP method, the GRG Nonlinear method, and the Evolutionary method. Each of these solving methods is discussed in detail as follows:

Determining Which of the 3 Solving Methods To Use

Simplex LP Method

Simplex LP is used to solve models that have only first-order equations. First-order mathematical equations are those that use the 4 most basic mathematical operations of addition, subtraction, multiplication, or division.

LP stand for Linear Programming. The Simplex LP method will be used if all of equations involving Decision Variables or Constraints are linear functions. Linear functions will produce a straight line when graphed.

The Simplex LP method will always produce a Globally Optimal Solution for optimization problems that it can solve. A Globally Optimal Solution is the best possibly solution which meets all Constraints.

The Simplex LP Solver always find the Globally Optimal Solution at the point where 2 or more Constraints intersect.

GRG Nonlinear Method

GRG Nonlinear should be selected if any of the equations involving Decision Variables or Constraints is nonlinear and smooth. GRG stands for Generalized Reduced Gradient and is a long-time, proven, reliable method for solving nonlinear problems. The GRG Nonlinear solving method works fine on linear problems as well, but takes longer and is less efficient for linear problems than the Simplex LP method.

Nonlinear equations most frequently occur as equations in which variables are taken to a power or to a root. Nonlinear equations produce nonlinear graphs. If any equation in the mathematical path to the Objective or in a Constraint contains a nonlinear variable such as a power or a root, you will have to select the GRG Nonlinear method.

Another requirement of the GRG Nonlinear method is that all equations involving Decision Variables or Constraints are smooth. An equation is "smooth" is that equation and the derivative of that equation has no breaks (is continuous).

One way to determine whether an equation or function is non-smooth (the graph has a sharp point indicating that the derivative is discontinuous) or discontinuous (the equation's graph abruptly changes value at certain points – the graph is disconnected at those points) is to graph the equation over its expected range of values.

When the Solver runs the GRG algorithm, it picks a starting point for its calculations. Each time you run the Solver GRG method on nonlinear equations, a slightly different starting point will be picked. That is why different answers will appear after each run. Re-run the Solver with the Decision Variable values that occurs during the run which produces the lowest or highest value of the Objective that you are seeking. Keep running the Solver until the objective is not minimized or maximized anymore. That should give you the optimal values of the Decision Variables. In the Nonlinear Regression example in this manual, the GRG Nonlinear method was run 2 successive times to obtain listed solution.

A process that produces different outputs for different runs is known as being nondeterministic.

The GRG Nonlinear Solver also has an option called Multistart which selects a number of different starting points, which produce a number of different Locally Optimal solutions. This increases the chance of arriving at a Globally Optimal solution.

The GRG Nonlinear Solver will produce a Globally Optimal solution if all functions in the Clear Mathematical Path to the Objective and all Constraints are convex. If any of the functions or Constraints are non-convex, the GRG Nonlinear Solver may find only Locally Optimal Solutions.

The GRG Nonlinear method can be used to solve any linear problem, but will do so much less efficiently than the Simplex LP method.

Evolutionary Method

The Evolutionary method must be used if any functions in the Clear Mathematical Path to the Objective is discontinuous or non-smooth. The Evolutionary method is so named because it uses Evolutionary algorithms when solving.

Non-smooth and discontinuous functions are often the most difficult optimization problems and can take much longer for the Excel Solver to solve. The Evolutionary method used to solve the Traveling Salesman example in this manual took 164 seconds to complete its job. You may view the problem's Answer Report see this run time.

Further, the Evolutionary method can often can only find a "good" solution and not a globally or locally optimal solution.

Common non-smooth Excel functions are MIN, MAX, and ABS.

Common discontinuous Excel functions are INDEX, HLOOKUP, VLOOKUP, LOOKUP, INT, ROUND, COUNT, CEILING, FLOOR, IF, CHOOSE, NOT AND, OR, GREATER THAN, LESS THAN, and EQUAL TO.

If any of the above functions or other non-smooth or discontinuous functions are in the Clear Mathematical Path to the Objective, the Evolutionary method must be used.

An example of the Evolutionary method in use is the Traveling Salesman Problem in this manual. The Evolutionary method had to be used in this example because the Clear Mathematical Path to the Objective contains the discontinuous Excel INDEX lookup function.

The Evolutionary method can be used to solve any problem can be solved with the GRG Nonlinear method or the Simplex LP method, but will do so much less efficiently.

A Solver Solution's 3 Possible Degrees of Optimality

Your completed Excel model should now be ready for the Solver to solve. Below is a description of the 3 possible types of optimal solutions that the Solver is able to provide:

1) **Globally Optimal** – A Globally Optimal solution is the best possible solution that meets all Constraints. A Globally Optimal solution might be comparable to Mount Everest since Mount Everest is the highest of all mountains.

2) **Locally Optimal** – A Locally Optimal solution is the best nearby solution that meets all constraints. It may not be the best overall solution, but it is best nearby solution. A Locally Optimal solution might be comparable to Mount McKinley, which is the highest mountain in North America but not the highest of all mountains.

3) **Good** – Non-convex, discontinuous, or non-smooth problems can often only be solved only to "good" solutions that have no guarantee of being even locally optimal. A "good" solution is the best **Feasible** solution that the Solver has found. Sometimes the Excel Solver will only be able to find **Feasible** solutions. A Feasible solution is one that merely satisfies all Constraints. A Feasible solution is not guaranteed to be an optimal one.

How Can You Try To Make a "Good" Solution Better?

A "good' solution will be 1 produced by the Evolutionary method. If you wish to improve on this solution, you may try the following techniques:

1) Re-run the Evolutionary method over again starting with that solution. It may produce a better solution.

2) Increase the Population Size and/or Mutation Rate and run the Evolutionary method again. This will increase the number of sample points that the Evolutionary method will explore, possibly resulting in a better solution.

3) Increase the allowable number of max Subproblems or max Feasible solutions in the All Methods Options box.

4) Try solving the same problem and same solution using the GRG Nonlinear method. If the GRG Nonlinear method finds a solution, you will know that this solution is at least a locally optimal solution and not just a good, feasible one.

Convex and Non-Convex Functions

A function's convexity determines what degree of optimality can be achieved by the Excel Solver.

A function is convex if it has only 1 peak, either up or down. A convex function can always be solved to a Globally Optimal solution.

A function is non-convex if it has more than 1 peak or it is discontinuous. The Sine, Cosine, and Tangent functions are good examples of non-convex functions. Non-convex functions can often be solved only to Locally Optimal solutions.

Solver Option Settings

Here are Solver settings that you want to configure prior to running the Solver for most problems. These settings are found when you click the Options button in the Solver dialogue box:

All Methods – Option Settings

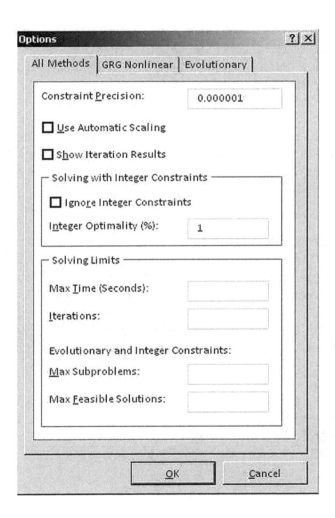

Constraint Precision: This establishes how close you want the value in any Constrained cell to be to the actual Constraint Value. The Constraint Precision value is maximum allowable difference between the value in a Constrained cell and the value of the actual Constraint. The Constraint is satisfied only if that difference is equal to or less than the Constraint Precision setting.

Use Automatic Scaling: This setting prompts the Solver to rescale variables, Constraints, and the Objective. You would use this option if you had reason to believe that inputs of the Solver were measured using different scales. The Objective, all Decision Variables, and all Constrained variables should be within no more than a few orders of magnitude of each other. A poorly scaled problem can result in a number of unexpected errors and stopping conditions.

Show Iteration Results: This stops the Solver after each trial run and displays the result for that iteration. In most cases you can leave this option unchecked unless you have a specific reason to view the results after each trial run.

Ignore Integer Constraints: These Integer Constraints are the Binary, Integer, and Alldifferent Constraints. Leave this unchecked unless you have a specific reason to override integer Constraints on the next trial run.

If you are unable to obtain a feasible solution and Integer Constraints have been applied, try relaxing them by checking this setting.

Integer Optimality (%): The maximum allowable percentage difference between the value of the best Integer solution and the value of the true Objective. The default is 1%. Setting this to 0% will ensure that the optimal solution is found, but will take longer to find.

Solving Limits

Max Time (Seconds): The maximum number of seconds that the Solver will be allowed to run. No matter what, the Solver can always be stopped by hitting the Esc key. At that point, you are given the option of Stopping or Restarting the Solver operation.

Iterations: The maximum number of iterations (trial runs) that the Solver will be allowed to perform.

Evolutionary and Integer Constraints – These apply only if the Evolutionary method is used or if any Integer Constraints (Integer, Binary, or Alldifferent) are used.

Max Subproblems The maximum number of subproblems that the Evolutionary method will be allowed to evaluate.

Max Feasible Solutions The maximum number of feasible solutions that the Solver will be allowed to generate.

GRG Nonlinear Option Settings

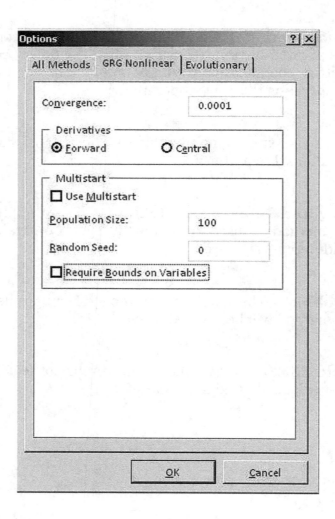

Convergence: The Convergence setting allows you to specify how close the final Solver solution must be to the optimal solution. Specifically, the Convergence setting establishes how small the percent change of the Objective between successive iterations must become over its last 5

iterations before the Solver will present the following message: "Solver converged to the current solution" and then its final solution.

The smaller the value, the more iterations must be run to reach that smaller convergence value, but Solver final solution will be closer to the optimal solution. To sum up, this setting tells how much the Objective must have slowed its changing during successive iterations for the Solver to finally announce that it has converged to a solution.

Derivatives: This setting establishes which type of finite differencing technique the Solver will use to approximate derivatives. Forward difference derivative approximations use less computing time but are not quite as accurate as central difference derivative approximations, which require twice as many calculations. Forward differencing is the default choice.

Multistart: The GRG Nonlinear Solver will produce a Globally Optimal solution when solving a convex, smooth, nonlinear problem. When dealing with a non-convex problem, the GRG Solver will produce only a Locally Optimal Solution This will be the closest peak or valley that resulted from the Decision Variable values that were initially supplied.

There are 2 ways to increase the chance that the Solver will arrive at a Globally Optimal solution:

The first is to run Solver multiple times using different sets of initial values for the Decision Variables. This option allows you to select sets of Decision Variables based on your understanding of the overall problem and is often the best way to arrive at the most desirable solution.

The second way is to select "Use Multistart." This runs the GRG Solver a number of times and randomly select a different set of initial values for the Decision Variables during each run. The Solver then presents the best of all of the Locally Optimal solutions that it has found.

One way to increase the chance of the multistart method locating the optimal solution is to select the final option "Require Bound on the Variables" and set boundaries on all of the Decision Variables using Constraints.

Running the multistart method takes significantly more processing time than a single run of the GRG Nonlinear Solver.

Population Size: This setting establishes how many times the multistart method should run until the GRG Nonlinear method presents the best of all of the Locally Optimal solutions that it has found. The Population Size is the number of sets of Decision Variable initial values that the GRG Nonlinear method will run through before providing its answer. This number should be between 10 and 200. A setting of less than 10 or blank will result in the minimum number of 10 multistart runs.

Random Seed: The GRG Nonlinear method uses a random number generator to select a starting point for Decision Variables. If this setting is left blank, the random number generator will generate different starting points for the Decision Variables every time the multistart method runs. This can produce a different solution on each different Solver run. To ensure that the same Decision Variable starting points are used each time Solve is hit, input a positive integer as the Random Seed.

Require Bounds On Variables: The multistart method is much more efficient if all Decision Variables are bound using Constraints. The tighter that these bounds are, the greater is the chance that the multistart method will produce the best Locally Optimal solution. Selecting this option will ensure that the multistart method will be employed only if all Decision Variables have their upper and lower values bound with Constraints.

Evolutionary Option Settings

```
Options                                          ? X
 All Methods | GRG Nonlinear | Evolutionary |

   Convergence:              0.0001|

   Mutation Rate:            0.075

   Population Size:          100

   Random Seed:             0

   Maximum Time without     30
   improvement:

   ☐ Require Bounds on Variables




                    OK              Cancel
```

Convergence: The Convergence setting allows you to specify how close the final Solver solution will be to the optimal solution. The Convergence setting establishes the maximum percentage difference that the last 99% of Solver trial answers (objective values) must be from each other before the Solver presents the following message: "Solver converged to the current solution" and provides its final solution. The smaller the value, the more iterations must be run to reach that smaller convergence value, but Solver final solution will be closer to the optimal solution.

Mutation Rate: The Evolutionary algorithm maintains a population of sample points in different regions of the search space. These sample points allow different and possibly better solutions to be found. The sample points are "mutated" by the Evolutionary algorithm at a specific frequency to increase the odds of locating the best solution. To establish or increase this frequency, set the Mutation Rate with a number between 0 and 1. This will determine the mutation frequency of each sample point during the successive generations, or subproblems, that are run through the Evolutionary method every time "Solve" is clicked.

Population Size: This setting establishes how many different sample points should be maintained as values for each Decision Variable at any given time. This number should be between 10 and 200. A setting of less than 10 or leaving the setting blank will result in the minimum number of 10 sample points being used for each Decision Variable.

Random Seed: The Evolutionary Solver uses a random number generator to perform a variety of random choices. If this setting is left blank, the random number generator will generate different choices every time the Evolutionary Solver is run. This can produce a different final solution for each different Solver run. To ensure that the Evolutionary Solver will use the same choices each time that "Solve" is clicked, input a positive integer as the Random Seed.

Maximum Time without Improvement This limits the maximum number of seconds that the Solver's Evolutionary method will continue its processing without meaningful improvement its final solution. After this interval has passed, the Solver will stop and delivery the following message: "Solver cannot improve the current solution." This setting will prevent the Evolutionary method from running for too long. The Traveling Salesman problem in this manual employed the Evolutionary method and took 164 seconds to provide its final solution. This time could have been greatly reduced if this setting had been set to a significantly shorter time period.

Require Bounds On Variables: The Evolutionary Solver is much more efficient if all Decision Variables are bound using Constraints. The tighter that these bounds are, the greater is the chance that the Evolutionary Solver will produce the best solution. Checking this option will ensure that the Evolutionary Solver will be employed only if all Decision Variables have their upper and lower values bound with Constraints.

Interpreting Solver Results Messages

Messages When Solver Encounters a Problem While Solving

Solver could not find a feasible solution.

The Solver was unable to find any combination of Decision Variables that satisfied all constraints. This error message is quite often caused by conflicting Constraints that cannot be satisfied simultaneously. The Feasibility Report is a good place to start looking for conflicting Constraints. This report will be made available in the Reports list box when this error occurs.

Using the Simplex LP method – This error message indicates with certainty that no feasible (simultaneously satisfying all Constraints) solution exists as long as the current model is properly scaled.

Using the GRG Nonlinear Method – No feasible solution could be found using the supplied Decision Variable values. It is still possible that a feasible solution might be found using different values for the Decision Variables.

Using the Evolutionary Method – No feasible solution could be found using the supplied Decision Variable values. It is still possible that a feasible solution might be found using different values for the Decision Variables. You might also try increasing the Constraint Precision setting in the All Methods Option dialogue box. Increasing this number reduces the precision with which the Constraints have to be satisfied, possibly allowing Decision Variable combinations to be accepted that might not have been accepted with the current tighter required precision.

Using Integer Constraints – If you are unable to obtain a feasible solution and Integer Constraints have been applied, try relaxing them by selecting the All Methods Options setting **Ignore Integer Constraints**.

The problem is too large for Solver to handle.

This error message indicates that the model either contains too many Decision Variables or too many constraints for the Excel Solver. 200 Decision Variables is the maximum number that Excel Solver allows for each of its 3 solving methods. The GRG Nonlinear and Evolutionary solving methods as used by the Excel Solver cannot process more than 100 Constraints in additional to upper and lower bounds for variables.

This error message would be a good indication that a more powerful optimization tool than the Excel Solver must be brought to bear on the problem. A good starting point to locate a more powerful Solver would be the creator of the original Excel Solver and the current world leader in optimization software development: Frontline Systems, Inc. Their web site is: http://www.solver.com/

The Objective Cell values do not converge.

This error message indicates that the Solver is able to increase or decrease the value in the Objective cell without limit while satisfying all Constraints. The most likely cause of this error is either that a necessary Constraint has not been included or some condition exists which allows the Objective cell to increase or decrease without limit.

Using the Simplex LP method – A Constraint has probably been forgotten.

Using the GRG Nonlinear method – A Constraint has probably been forgotten.

Using the Evolutionary method – This error message will never appear when the Evolutionary method is used.

One tip is to check whether the Constraint **Make Unconstrained Variables Non-Negative** has been left unchecked but should be checked. This ensures that Decision Variables can never be negative.

The linearity conditions required by this LP Solver are not satisfied.

This message appears only when using the Simplex LP method. It indicates that a Constraint, function, or formula in the Clear Mathematical Math to the Objective is nonlinear. The Simplex LP method requires all formulas in the Clear Mathematical Path to the Objective to be linear.

The Linearity Report is a good place to begin troubleshooting when this error message occurs. The Linearity Report is made available in the Reports list box when this error appears. The Linearity Report will point out any formulas for the Constraints and variables in the Clear Mathematical Path to the Objective that are nonlinear or non-smooth.

Solver encountered an error value in the objective cell or a constraint cell.

This message indicates that an error somewhere in the model has produced an error value in the Objective cell or a Constraint cell such as #NAME?, #DIV/o!, #VALUE!, or #NUM!.

Errors such as #N/A, #NAME?, or #VALUE! often indicate a reference to a cell that has been moved or deleted.

Errors such as #DIV/o! or #NUM! often indicate that a Decision Variable was assigned an unanticipated value by Solver. Most likely this situation will require an additional Constraint to be added in order to limit the value of the Decision Variable.

If this error occurs while using the GRG Nonlinear method, try switching to the Evolutionary method. The Evolutionary method rarely displays this error message. If a trial run of the Evolutionary method produces this error, the Evolutionary method simply discards that combination of Decision Variables and tries another one. The Evolutionary method should at least be able to find a "good" solution for a nonlinear problem.

This message appears when Solver recalculates the worksheet using a new set of values for the Decision Variable cells and discovers an error value such as #VALUE!, #NUM!, #DIV/0! or #NAME? in the Objective cell or one of the Constraint cells. Inspect the worksheet for error values like these to locate the source of the problem.

Another cause of this error is a Constraint with formulas written on the right side. **<u>Always ensure that Constraints have formulas on the left side and constant numbers or cell containing constant values on the right side.</u>**

This error might also be caused by a Constraint with a 0 on the right side. You can sometimes solve this error by rewriting, for example, Constraint $B5$1 >= 0 to this Constraint: $B$5 >= 0.001.

There is not enough memory available to solve the problem.

This error message is unlikely to appear today because of the increased power of modern computers. Solver processing times would greatly increase before this error would appear.

Messages When Solver Found a Problem With Constraints

All variables must have both upper and lower bounds.

This error indicates that Constraints have not been set which limit the upper or lower values of at least one Decision Variable. If you are running the Evolutionary method or the Multistart method with the GRG Nonlinear method and you have checked the option **Require Bounds on Variables**, all Decision Variables are required to have Constraints which limit their upper and lower values.

Evaluate the Constraints to see which Decision Variable needs an additional upper or lower bound created.

One way to limit the lower bounds of all Decision Variables to 0 is the check the **Make Unconstrained Variables Non-Negative** check box

Variable bounds conflict in binary or alldifferent constraint.

This error message indicates that one variable is Constrained both by a binary or all different Constraint and also with a conflicting bounding Constraint of <= or >=. Binary variables have upper and lower values of 1 and 0. A group of variables Constrained by the Alldifferent Constraint have a lower bound of 1 and an upper bound of N, which is the number of variables in the group. Any Constraint of <= or >=. must be in agreement with the upper and lower bounds of the Binary and Alldifferent Constraints.

Lower and upper bounds on variables allow no feasible solution.

This error message indicates that a variable's upper bound is lower than its lower bound.

Messages When Solver Finds a Solution

Solver found a solution. All constraints and optimality conditions are satisfied.

This message indicates that the Solver has found the best solution that it can for the specific type of problem.

<u>**Using the Simplex LP method**</u> – The solution is a Globally Optimal solution.

<u>**Using the GRG Nonlinear method for smooth nonlinear problems with no integer constraints**</u> (Integer, Binary, or Alldifferent) – The solution is a Locally Optimal solution. Different initial values for the Decision Variables might produce a different and possibly better result.

<u>**Using the GRG Nonlinear method for smooth nonlinear problems WITH integer constraints**</u> – The solution is the best of all of the Locally Optimal solutions found.

<u>**Using the Evolutionary method**</u> – This message will not appear when using this solving method.

Solver has converged to the current solution. All constraints are satisfied.

This message appears when the Solver has run multiple iterations and has narrowed down (converged) its answer to within acceptable limits. The exact definition of this message depends on which Solver method is being used.

<u>**Using Simplex LP method**</u> – This message does not appear when using this method.

<u>Using the GRG Nonlinear method to solve a smooth nonlinear problem</u> – This method will provide its final solution and present this message when the last 5 iterations produce a smaller percent change the Objective function than the Convergence setting in the GRG Nonlinear section of the Solver Options dialogue box. The smaller the value of this Convergence setting, the more iterations must be run to reach that smaller convergence value, but the Solver final solution will be closer to the optimal solution.

<u>Using the Evolutionary method for a non-smooth problem</u> - This method will provide its final solution and present this message when the 99% of the most recent Objective function answers have a maximum percent difference less than the Convergence setting in the Evolutionary section of the Solver Options dialogue box. The smaller the value of this Convergence setting, the more iterations must be run to reach that smaller convergence value, but the Solver final solution will be closer to the optimal solution.

If you are not getting convergence, trying increasing the value of Convergence setting in order to loosen the required convergence difference. Another possible solution might be to increase the Mutation Rate and/or the Population Size in order to increase the diversity of the population of trial solutions.

Solver cannot improve the current solution. All constraints are satisfied.

This message means that the Solver has found a solution that satisfies the Constraints but does not satisfy the Solver's tests for optimality and convergence. The exact definition of this message depends which Solver method is being used.

<u>Using Simplex LP method</u> – This message does not appear when using this Solver.

<u>Using the GRG Nonlinear method to solve a smooth nonlinear problem</u> – This message does not appear often when using the GRG Nonlinear Solver. When it does, it probably indicates that the model has flaws which cause continuous cycling. The most likely reasons for this are redundant Constraints.

<u>Using the Evolutionary method for a non-smooth problem</u> - This message means that the Solver has not found a solution that satisfies the Constraints but has not satisfied the Convergence setting in the Evolutionary section of the Solver Options dialogue box within the time limit set in the Maximum Time without Improvement setting. You can increase this Maximum Time setting to allow the Solver to run longer. This may produce a more optimal answer. You can also loosen the Convergence setting.

Solver found an integer solution within tolerance. All constraints are satisfied.

This message can occur when solving any problem with integer Constraints (Integer, Binary, or Alldifferent Constraints) and there is a non-zero in the **Integer Optimality %** setting in the All Methods section of the Solver Options dialogue box.

This message indicates that the Solver has found a solution in which the percentage difference between the solution and the true Objective value does not exceed the Integer Optimality % setting and also satisfies all Constraints.

Solver converged in probability to a global solution.
This message can occur when using the multistart method within the GRG Nonlinear method. This message indicates that the solution found is probably a Globally Optimal solution. The Solver has determined that all of the Locally Optimal solutions have probably been found and therefore the best of all of the Locally Optimal solutions being presented is probably the Globally Optimal solution.

Messages When ESC Is Pressed or a Solving Limit Is Reached

Solver stopped at user's request.

This message will appear only when you press ESC to display the Show Trial Solution dialog, and then hit the Stop button. No reports will shown in the Results dialog.

Stop chosen when the maximum time limit was reached.

This message occurs when the Solver has run to the limit of the time allowed in the Maximum Time setting in the All Methods section of the Options Solver dialogue box. This message also occurs when Stop is selected when Solver displays the Show Trial Solution dialogue box.

Stop chosen when the maximum iteration limit was reached.

This message occurs when the Solver has processed the maximum number of iterations allowed in the Iterations setting in the All Methods section of the Options Solver dialogue box. This message also occurs when Stop is selected when Solver displays the Show Trial Solution dialogue box.

Stop chosen when the maximum number of [integer] subproblems was reached.

This message can occur if a problem has integer Constraints (Integer, Binary, or Alldifferent Constraint) or if a problem is being solved with the Evolutionary method. This message indicates that the Solver has run the maximum number of subproblems allowed in the **Maximum Subproblems** setting in the All Methods section of the Options Solver dialogue box. This message also occurs when Stop is selected after Solver displays the Show Trial Solution dialogue box.

Understanding Solver Reports

Solver makes reports available when the following 2 events occur:

1) Solver find a solution.
2) A problem arises during a Solver run.

Reports Made Available When the Solver Finds a Solution

At least 1 of these 4 reports are made available each time the Solver finds a solution. These 4 reports are made available individually in the following circumstances:

Answer Report – The Answer Report is almost always made available immediately after the Solver find a solution. Specifically, the Answer Report is made available when the Solver finds an optimal solution, converges to a solution, or cannot improve the solution further.

Population Report – The Population Report is made available when the Evolutionary method is used.

Limits Report – The Limits Report is made available when the Solver finds a Globally or Locally Optimal solution and no Integer Constraints (Integer, Binary, Alldifferent) were used.

Sensitivity Report – The Sensitivity Report is also made available when the Solver finds a Globally or Locally Optimal solution and no Integer Constraints (Integer, Binary, Alldifferent) were used.

Reports Made Available In Certain Situations When a Problem Occurs During a Solver Run

Linearity Report – The Linearity Report is made available when the Simplex LP method is used and a nonlinear formula occurs in the Clear Mathematical Path to the Objective or in a Constraint. The Simplex LP method requires that all formulas in the Clear Mathematical Path to the Objective and in Constraints be linear (first order).

Feasibility Report – The Feasibility Report is made available when no feasible solution (one that satisfies all of the Constraints) can be found and no Integer Constraints (Integer, Binary, Alldifferent) were used. This report indicates which Constraints cannot be satisfied and therefore cause the infeasibility condition. Both this report and the Feasibility-Bounds Report indicate what is causing the infeasibility condition. Only one of these two reports needs to be examined to determine the source of infeasibility.

Feasibility-Bounds Report – The Feasibility-Bounds Report is also made available when no feasible solution (one that satisfies all of the Constraints) can be found and no Integer Constraints (Integer, Binary, Alldifferent) were used. This report indicates which Constraints cannot be satisfied and therefore cause the infeasibility condition. Both this report and Feasibility Report indicate what is causing the infeasibility condition. Only one of these two reports needs to be examined to determine the source of infeasibility.

Reports Made Available When the Solver Finds a Solution

The Answer Report and How To Read It

The Answer Report is made available when the Solver finds an optimal solution, converges to a solution, or cannot improve the solution further. An example of an Answer report shown below.

Here are the 3 parts of the Answer Report generated for the Purchase-Transportation problem in this manual:

Answer Report - Part 1 – Objective Cell

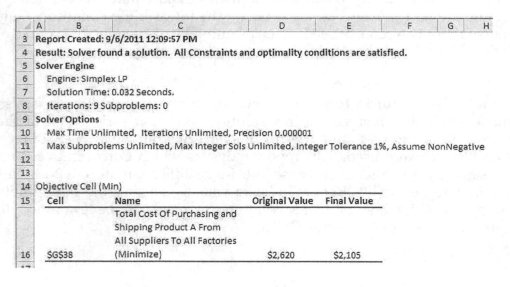

	A	B	C	D	E	F	G	H
3	Report Created: 9/6/2011 12:09:57 PM							
4	Result: Solver found a solution. All Constraints and optimality conditions are satisfied.							
5	Solver Engine							
6	Engine: Simplex LP							
7	Solution Time: 0.032 Seconds.							
8	Iterations: 9 Subproblems: 0							
9	Solver Options							
10	Max Time Unlimited, Iterations Unlimited, Precision 0.000001							
11	Max Subproblems Unlimited, Max Integer Sols Unlimited, Integer Tolerance 1%, Assume NonNegative							
12								
13								
14	Objective Cell (Min)							
15	Cell	Name		Original Value	Final Value			
16	$G$38	Total Cost Of Purchasing and Shipping Product A From All Suppliers To All Factories (Minimize)		$2,620	$2,105			

Solver Result – The message that appears in the Solver dialogue box as soon as the Solver has found a solution and states what kind of result the Solver found.

Solver Engine – The type of Solver method that was used (Simplex LP, GRG Nonlinear, or Evolutionary method)

Solution time – The total time it took the Solver to find the solution. Some problems take quite a bit more time than others. Most Simplex LP problems are solved quickly. Note that the Answer Report for the Traveling Salesman problem shows that the Evolutionary Solver took 164 seconds to reach its solution because it had to run through 123,302 subproblems. This run time could have been limited by applying options settings.

Number of Iterations or Subproblems that the Solver had to run in order to reach the given solution.

Solver Options – The settings of all options available when the Options button is clicked in the Solver Dialogue box.

Objective Cell – The type of Objective, the location of the Objective cell, the name of the Objective cell, the original value appearing in the Objective cell before running Solver, and the final solution that the Solver has arrived at.

The name of the Objective cell will be the first label that the Solver finds directly above the Objective cell. If you are putting the Objective cell's name under the Objective cell instead of putting the name directly over top of the Objective cell, the cell name will likely be mislabeled on the Answer Report.

Care was taken when creating the Excel examples in this manual to place the label for the Objective cell in the correct place so that it would appear correctly on the Answer Report. Take a look at how the labels appear on the Excel spreadsheet for each problem and how the cell naming results appear in that problem's Answer Report.

Answer Report - Part 2 - Decision Variables

	Cell	Name	Original Value	Final Value	Integer
19	Variable Cells				
20	Cell	Name	Original Value	Final Value	Integer
21	$C$20	Factory 1 Units from Supplier 1	10	0	Integer
22	$C$21	Factory 2 Units from Supplier 1	10	0	Integer
23	$C$22	Factory 3 Units from Supplier 1	10	40	Integer
24	$C$23	Factory 4 Units from Supplier 1	10	0	Integer
25	$D$20	Factory 1 Units from Supplier 2	10	5	Integer
26	$D$21	Factory 2 Units from Supplier 2	10	10	Integer
27	$D$22	Factory 3 Units from Supplier 2	10	0	Integer
28	$D$23	Factory 4 Units from Supplier 2	10	0	Integer

	A	B	C	D	E	F
28		$D$23	Factory 4 Units from Supplier 2	10	0	Integer
29		$E$20	Factory 1 Units from Supplier 3	10	0	Integer
30		$E$21	Factory 2 Units from Supplier 3	10	20	Integer
31		$E$22	Factory 3 Units from Supplier 3	10	0	Integer
32		$E$23	Factory 4 Units from Supplier 3	10	0	Integer
33		$F$20	Factory 1 Units from Supplier 4	10	15	Integer
34		$F$21	Factory 2 Units from Supplier 4	10	0	Integer
35		$F$22	Factory 3 Units from Supplier 4	10	0	Integer
36		$F$23	Factory 4 Units from Supplier 4	10	50	Integer

Variable Cells (Decision Variables) – 1) The location of each decision variable, 2) the name that first appear in the cells directly above each Decision Variable on the spreadsheet, 3) the original value of the Decision Variable before Solver is run, 4) the Decision Variable's final value after Solver has found a solution, 5) and the type of value this Decision Variable is (Continuous, Integer, Binary, Alldifferent).

The Name of the Variable Cell will be taken from the nearest label over the top of the Decision Variable or by combining the nearest label directly to the left of the Decision Variable along with the nearest label on top of that Decision Variable. Part 2 of the Answer Report in the Outbound Marketing example in this manual provides an illustration of this second naming convention.

Answer Report - Part 3 – Constraints

	A	B	C	D	E	F	G
38							
39	Constraints						
40		Cell	Name	Cell Value	Formula	Status	Slack
41		$C$25	Total Number of Units Purchased From Supplier A	40	$C$25<=$C$52	Not Binding	60
42		$D$25	Total Number of Units Purchased From Supplier B	15	$D$25<=$C$54	Binding	0
43		$E$25	Total Number of Units Purchased From Supplier C	20	$E$25<=$C$56	Binding	0
44		$F$25	Total Number of Units Purchased From Supplier D	65	$F$25<=$C$58	Not Binding	85
45		$G$20	Factory 1 Total Units Received	20	$G$20=$C$42	Binding	0
46		$G$21	Factory 2 Total Units Received	30	$G$21=$C$44	Binding	0
47		$G$22	Factory 3 Total Units Received	40	$G$22=$C$46	Binding	0
48		$G$23	Factory 4 Total Units Received	50	$G$23=$C$48	Binding	0

	A	B	C	D	E	F	G
47		$G$22	Factory 3 Total Units Received	40	$G$22=$C$46	Binding	0
48		$G$23	Factory 4 Total Units Received	50	$G$23=$C$48	Binding	0
49		$C$20=Integer					
50		$C$21=Integer					
51		$C$22=Integer					
52		$C$23=Integer					
53		$D$20=Integer					
54		$D$21=Integer					
55		$D$22=Integer					
56		$D$23=Integer					
57		$E$20=Integer					
58		$E$21=Integer					
59		$E$22=Integer					
60		$E$23=Integer					
61		$F$20=Integer					
62		$F$21=Integer					
63		$F$22=Integer					
64		$F$23=Integer					

Constraints – 1) The location of each cell containing a variable value that has a Constraint applied to it, 2) the name that first appear in the cells directly above each Constrained cell, the final value in the Constrained cell after Solver has found a solution, 3) the Excel formula in the Solver dialogue box creating that Constraint, 4) whether that Constraint is binding or nonbinding, 5) and the amount of slack that the value of a nonbinding cell has until it hits its Constraint limit.

Listing a Constrained value as binding means that this Constraint's limit was reached during the Solver run. Being listed as Nonbinding means that the Constraint's value was not hit. Slack equals the amount of available room that each nonbinding variable still has after Solver has found a solution. This is the different between that Constrained cell's final value and the upper or lower limit imposed by the Constraint.

The Population Report and How To Read It

The Population Report is made available when the Evolutionary method is used. The Population Report provides indication about whether and how you can make improvements to the model or to the Evolutionary method Options.

Here is the Population Report generated for the Traveling Salesman problem in this manual:

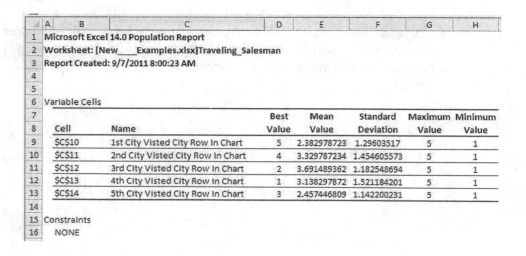

	A	B	C	D	E	F	G	H
1	Microsoft Excel 14.0 Population Report							
2	Worksheet: [New____Examples.xlsx]Traveling_Salesman							
3	Report Created: 9/7/2011 8:00:23 AM							
4								
5								
6	Variable Cells							
7				Best	Mean	Standard	Maximum	Minimum
8	Cell	Name		Value	Value	Deviation	Value	Value
9	$C$10	1st City Visted City Row In Chart		5	2.382978723	1.29603517	5	1
10	$C$11	2nd City Visted City Row In Chart		4	3.329787234	1.454605573	5	1
11	$C$12	3rd City Visted City Row In Chart		2	3.691489362	1.182548694	5	1
12	$C$13	4th City Visted City Row In Chart		1	3.138297872	1.521184201	5	1
13	$C$14	5th City Visted City Row In Chart		3	2.457446809	1.142200231	5	1
14								
15	Constraints							
16	NONE							

The Population Report provides the following information about each Decision Variable and each Constraint:

Cell Location of each Decision Variable and each Constrained variable.

Name - The Name of the Variable Cell will be taken from the nearest label over the top of the Decision Variable or by combining the nearest label directly to the left of the Decision Variable along with the nearest label on top of that Decision Variable. Part 2 of the Answer Report in the

Outbound Marketing example in this manual provides an illustration of this second naming convention.

Best Value – The value that the Solver assigned to that Decision Variable during the Solver run which calculated the current Objective solution.

Mean Value – The mean value of the entire population of available candidate solutions for a particular Decision Variable or Constraint.

Standard Deviation – The standard deviation of the entire population of available candidate solutions for a particular Decision Variable or Constraint.

Minimum and Maximum Values – The minimum and maximum values of the entire population of available candidate solutions for particular Decision Variable or Constraint.

The Population Report provides an indication of whether or not you can further improve your solution with additional runs of the Evolutionary method at different Options settings.

It is important to note that the Evolutionary method can be counted on to yield only "good" results and not locally or globally optimal solutions. The Population Report indicates that you may have found an optimal solution when Standard Deviations are consistently small and Best Values are similar following multiple successive Solver Evolutionary method runs.

If Best Values vary significantly but Standard Deviation is consistently small after multiple successive runs, the collection of sample points evaluated by the Solver may not be diverse enough. Sample point diversity can be expanded by increasing the Mutation Rate in the Options settings.

The sample points are "mutated" by the Evolutionary algorithm at a specific frequency to increase the odds of locating the best solution. To increase this frequency, increase the Mutation Rate with a number between 0 and 1. The Mutation Rate determines the mutation frequency of each sample point during successive generations, or subproblems, that are run through the Evolutionary Solver every time "Solve" is clicked.

Another possibility for improving your Evolutionary method solution is to experiment with different Population Size settings in the Options menu. Population Size establishes how many sample points should be maintained as values for each Decision Variable at any given time. Vary the Population Size and examine the Population Report from each successive run for indications about whether the successive solutions are approaching optimality.

Optimality is evidenced when successive Solver Evolutionary runs produce consistently small Standard Deviations and smaller and smaller variation in Best Values.

An additional possibility for a more optimal solution with the Evolutionary method is to increase the Options setting "Maximum Time Without Improvement." Evaluate whether increasing that time reduces Standard Deviation and variation in Best Values on the Population Report.

One further tip when using the Evolutionary method is to apply upper and lower bounds to each Decision Variable using Constraints and then check the setting **Require Bounds on Variables**. The Evolutionary method will run much more efficiently when upper and lower bounds are applied to all Decision Variables.

The Limits Report and How To Read It

Limits Report – The Limits Report is made available when the Solver finds a Globally or Locally Optimal solution and no Integer Constraints (Integer, Binary, Alldifferent) were used.

The Limits Report is relatively straight-forward to interpret. It lists the upper and lower limits that each Decision Variable can take if the Objective and all other Decision Variables are held constant. The Limits Report indicates how much slack each Decision Variable has.

The Limits Reports from the Bond Portfolio example in this manual is shown as follows. The first section shows the Objective cell, its label, and its optimal value found by the Solver.

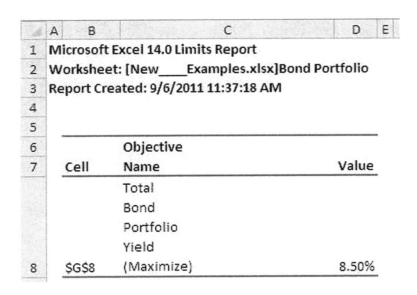

The 2nd section of the Limits Report shown as follows indicates that none of the Decision Variables have any slack because the upper and lower limits of each Decision Variable are the same.

	Cell	Variable Name	Value	Lower Limit	Objective Result	Upper Limit	Objective Result
13	$E$3	Bond 1 Portfolio Percentage	0%	0%	8.50%	0%	8.50%
14	$E$4	Bond 2 Portfolio Percentage	0%	0%	8.50%	0%	8.50%
15	$E$5	Bond 3 Portfolio Percentage	83%	83%	8.50%	83%	8.50%
16	$E$6	Bond 4 Portfolio Percentage	17%	17%	8.50%	17%	8.50%

The 3rd section of the Answer Report provides a similar analysis, but on the Constraints. This section of the Answer Report indicates how much slack each Constraint has.

The Sensitivity Report and How To Read It

The Sensitivity Report is made available when the Solver finds a Globally or Locally Optimal solution and no Integer Constraints (Integer, Binary, Alldifferent) were used. This report provides sensitivity analysis for both linear and nonlinear problems.

The Sensitivity Report requires an understanding of the concept of "Dual Values."

The Sensitivity Report for the Bond Portfolio example in this manual is provide here.

In Part 1 of the Sensitivity Report, the Dual Values for Decision Variables are shown in the column entitled "Reduced Cost" (for linear problems) or "Reduced Gradient" (for nonlinear problems).

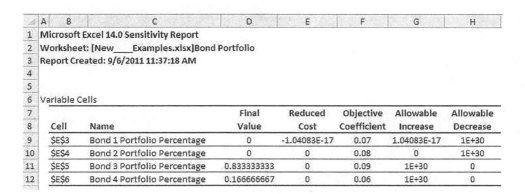

	Cell	Name	Final Value	Reduced Cost	Objective Coefficient	Allowable Increase	Allowable Decrease
		Microsoft Excel 14.0 Sensitivity Report					
		Worksheet: [New____Examples.xlsx]Bond Portfolio					
		Report Created: 9/6/2011 11:37:18 AM					
6	Variable Cells						
9	$E$3	Bond 1 Portfolio Percentage	0	-1.04083E-17	0.07	1.04083E-17	1E+30
10	$E$4	Bond 2 Portfolio Percentage	0	0	0.08	0	1E+30
11	$E$5	Bond 3 Portfolio Percentage	0.833333333	0	0.09	1E+30	0
12	$E$6	Bond 4 Portfolio Percentage	0.166666667	0	0.06	1E+30	0

The Dual Value for a Decision Variable equals zero unless that Decision Variable's final value is equal to its upper or lower bound. A Decision Variable's Dual Value (Reduced Cost or Reduced Gradient) is nonzero only when its final solution value equals its upper or lower bound. A nonzero Dual Value for a Decision Variable indicates that the Objective's final, optimal solution can be improved by loosening the binding Constraint on that Decision Variable.

Part 1 of the Sensitivity Report also shows each Decision Variable's coefficient in the Objective Function. Part 1 further shows how much this coefficient could be changed (increased or decreased) without changing its Dual Value (Reduced Cost for linear problems or Reduced Gradient for nonlinear problems).

In Part 2 of the Sensitivity Report, Dual Values for Constraints are shown in the column entitled "Shadow Price" (for linear problems) or "Lagrange Multipliers" (for nonlinear problems). The "Shadow Price" or "LaGrange Multipliers" tell how much Objective would improve for each unit of change in that Constraint.

In this example the overall portfolio return would increased by 1% (0.01) if a single year were added to the allowable average duration. In other words, if the portfolio duration were increased from 5.5 years to 6.5 years, the overall portfolio return would rise by 1%.

	A	B	C	D	E	F	G	H
13								
14		Constraints						
15				Final	Shadow	Constraint	Allowable	Allowable
16		Cell	Name	Value	Price	R.H. Side	Increase	Decrease
17		$E$8	Total Portfolio Held (Should Add Up To 100%)	1	0.03	1	0.833333333	0.083333333
18		$F$8	Total Target Bond Portfolio Duration (Years)	5.5	0.01	5.5	0.5	2.5

A Dual Value for a Constraint equals zero if that Constraint is nonbinding. A nonbinding Constraint is a Constraint whose limit has not been reached when the Solver arrives at its final, best solution. A Dual Value for a Constraint is nonzero if the Constraint is a binding Constraint. A nonzero Dual Value for a Constraint indicates that the

Objective's final, best solution can be improved by loosening that Constraint.

The Dual Value for a Constraint indicates how sensitive the problem is to changes in that Constraint. Specifically, a Constraint's Dual value (Shadow Price or Lagrange Multiplier) states how much the Objective function's value (final best solution) will change for each unit of change in that Constraint's bound.

For each Constraint, Part 2 of the Sensitivity Report shows the Constraint's Right Hand Side, which is the Constraint's limiting value. Part 2 also shows how much that Right Hand Side could be changed (increased or decreased) without affecting that Constraint's Dual Value (Shadow Price or Lagrange Multiplier).

For linear problems, Dual Values remain constant for a range of possible changes in the Objective function coefficients and Constraint right hand sides. This range information is provided in the Sensitivity report.

For nonlinear problems, the Dual Values provided are valid only at the optimal point. These values change as soon as you move away from the optimal solution because of the nonlinear problem's curvature.

Reports Made Available In Certain Situations When a Problem Occurs During a Solver Run

The Linearity Report and How To Read It

The Linearity Report is made available when the Simplex LP method is used and a nonlinear formula occurs somewhere in the Clear Mathematical Path to the Objective or in a Constraint. The Simplex LP method requires that all formulas in the Clear Mathematical Path to the Objective and in all Constraints be linear (first order).

If your model contains nonlinear formulas in the Clear Mathematical Path to the Objective or in a Constraint, you will have to use one of the other 2 methods (GRG Nonlinear or Evolutionary) to solve the problem.

We will illustrate an example of trying to use the Simplex LP method to solve a nonlinear formula with the Knapsack problem in this manual. We will change 1 of the formulas in the Knapsack example from linear to nonlinear and then attempt to solve it with the Simplex LP method. The Linearity Report will be generated as a result of this error.

Shown on the following page is the original Excel model for the Knapsack problem. All formulas in this model are linear and solvable with the Simplex LP method.

	Object	Number of Objects	Calories		Protein (grams)		Weight of Object (kg)		Volume of Object (m³)	
			Per Object	Total	Per Object	Total	Per Object	Total	Per Object	Total
4	Candy Bar	5	90	450	5	25	0.25	1.25	0.0005	0.003
5	Sandwich	25	130	3250	40	1000	0.35	8.75	0.002	0.050
6	Juice Can	0	100	0	15	0	0.35	0	0.00075	0.000
7	Apple	0	40	0	3	0	0.3	0	0.0009	0.000
8		Decision Variables	Total Calories (Maximize)		Total Protein (g)		Total Weight (kg)		Total Volume (m³)	
9	Column Totals		3700		1025		10		0.0525	
10			Objective		Constraint		Constraint		Constraint	

We then make a change to Objective cell, E9. Cell E9 contains the sum of the 4 Total Calorie figures directly above it. Raising 1 of those Total Calorie figures (cell C6 – the Decision Variable indicating the number of Juice Cans to be placed in the Knapsack) to the 3rd power while inside of the sum formula in cell E9 changes that formula from linear to nonlinear. This is illustrated in the updated Excel model shown as follows:

	Object	Number of Objects	Calories		Protein (grams)		Weight of Object (kg)		Volume of Object (m³)	
			Per Object	Total	Per Object	Total	Per Object	Total	Per Object	Total
4	Candy Bar	10	90	900	5	50	0.25	2.5	0.0005	0.005
5	Sandwich	10	130	1300	40	400	0.35	3.5	0.002	0.020
6	Juice Can	10	100	1000	15	150	0.35	3.5	0.00075	0.008
7	Apple	10	40	400	3	30	0.3	3	0.0009	0.009
8		Decision Variables	Total Calories (Maximize)		Total Protein (g)		Total Weight (kg)		Total Volume (m³)	
9			1000002600		630		12.5		0.0415	
10			Objective Cell E9 = E4+E5+E6^3+E7 (Taking the Contents of Cell E6 To the 3rd Power Creates a Nonlinear Condition)		Constraint		Constraint		Constraint	

Trying to solve this model, which now has a nonlinear formula in cell E9, with the Simplex LP generates the following Linearity Report. The Linearity Report has 3 parts.

Part 1 of the Linearity Report correctly identifies the Objective cell, E9, as containing a nonlinear formula.

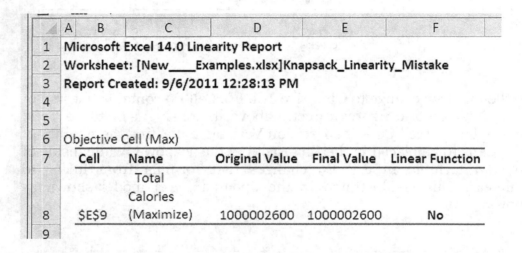

	A	B	C	D	E	F
1	Microsoft Excel 14.0 Linearity Report					
2	Worksheet: [New____Examples.xlsx]Knapsack_Linearity_Mistake					
3	Report Created: 9/6/2011 12:28:13 PM					
4						
5						
6	Objective Cell (Max)					
7		Cell	Name	Original Value	Final Value	Linear Function
8		$E$9	Total Calories (Maximize)	1000002600	1000002600	No
9						

Part 2 of the Linearity Report correctly identifies the Decision Variable in cell C6 (the number of Juice Cans to put in the Knapsack) is a Decision Variable that occurs in nonlinearly in the model.

	A	B	C	D	E	F	
11	Variable Cells						
12		Cell	Name	Original Value	Final Value	Occurs Linearly	
13		$C$4	Candy Bar Number of Objects	10	10	Yes	
14		$C$5	Sandwich Number of Objects	10	10	Yes	
15		$C$6	Juice Can Number of Objects	10	10	No	
16		$C$7	Apple Number of Objects	10	10	Yes	
17							

Part 3 of the Linearity Report finds no part of any Constraint to contain nonlinear formulas.

	Cell	Name	Cell Value	Formula	Linear Function
17					
18					
19	Constraints				
20	Cell	Name	Cell Value	Formula	Linear Function
21	$G$9	Total Protein (g)	630	$G$9>=$B$18	Yes
22	$I$9	Total Weight (kg)	12.5	$I$9<=$B$14	Yes
23	$K$9	Total Volume (m3)	0.0415	$K$9<=$B$16	Yes

One further solution that will enable the Simplex LP method to be used to solve nonlinear problems is to convert any nonlinear formula to its linear equivalent. You can then continue to use the Simplex LP method to solve the problem. Linear problems are generally solved much faster than nonlinear problems. This is especially true if the problem contains any integer Constraints (Integer, Binary, or Alldifferent). Converting nonlinear formulas to their linear equivalents is an advanced topic that will not be covered in this manual.

The Feasibility Report and How To Read It

The Feasibility Report is made available when no feasible solution (one that satisfies all of the Constraints) can be found and no Integer Constraints (Integer, Binary, Alldifferent) were used. This report indicates which Constraints cannot be satisfied and therefore cause the infeasibility condition. Both this report and Feasibility-Bounds Report indicate what is causing the infeasibility condition. Only one of these two reports needs to be examined to determine the source of infeasibility.

An infeasibility condition typically occurs when alimit of at least 1 Constraint or Decision Variable bound is reached before at least 1 other Constraint or Decision Variable bound has been satisfied. The Feasibility Report identifies the subset of limiting Constraints or Decision Variable bounds that are preventing other Constraints or Decision Variable bounds from being satisfied.

The Solver does a complete analysis of the model when infeasibility conditions occur. This can use up significant computing resources and time. You can interrupt the Feasibility Report computations by hitting the ESC key.

Below is an example of an infeasible condition which causes the Feasibility Report to be generated. We are using the Bond Portfolio problem from this manual. The original Excel model for this problem with no infeasibility condition is shown as follows:

	A	B	C	D	E	F	G
1					Decision Variables		
2			Bond Duration (Years)	Bond Yield	Portfolio Percentage	Duration X Portfolio Percentage	Yield X Portfolio Percentage
3		Bond 1	4	7%	0%	0	0.00%
4		Bond 2	5	8%	0%	0	0.00%
5		Bond 3	6	9%	83%	5	7.50%
6		Bond 4	3	6%	17%	0.5	1.00%
7					Total Portfolio Held (Should Add Up To 100%)	Total Target Bond Portfolio Duration (Years)	Total Bond Portfolio Yield (Maximize)
8					100%	5.5	8.50%
						Constraint	Objective

The original Solver dialogue box for this example shown as follows. It contains the correct Constraints that will produce a feasible solution.

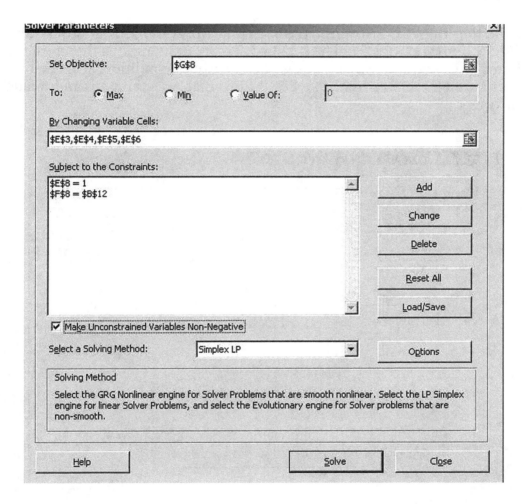

The 2nd Solver dialogue box shown as follows is the same Solver dialogue box as the original, except with one of the Constraints changed to produce an infeasible condition.

Note that the 1st Constraint ($E$8 = 1) now prevents the 2nd Constraint ($F$8 = $B$12*100) from be satisfied. The 1st Constraint is therefore the limiting Constraint which causes the infeasible condition. This is true even though it was the 2nd Constraint that was altered and made incorrect.

When "Solve" is clicked in the Solver dialogue box, the infeasibility condition will occur and the Feasibility Report shown as follows will be made available. The 1st Constraint is shown to be the binding Constraint (its limit has been reached) that prevented by the 2nd Constraint from being satisfied.

It is important to note that the Constraint or Decision Variable bound that is identified by the Feasibility Report is not necessarily the underlying error. In this example, the 1st Constraint is identified here by this report as the limiting Constraint that could not be met and therefore the source of infeasibility. The 1st Constraint does not, however, have the mistake in it. The 2nd Constraint was changed to be incorrect and create the error the infeasibility condition in the 1st Constraint. The 1st Constraint was the 1 that could not be met and was therefore identified in the Feasibility Report. The 2nd Constraint was the Constraint incorrectly written with the error.

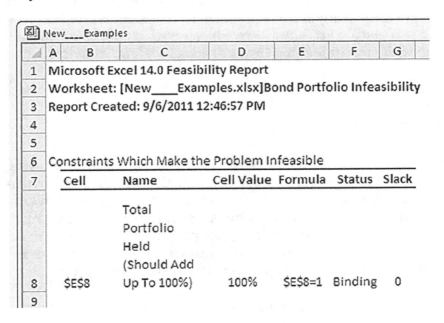

The **Feasibility Bounds Report** produces a similar output but does not attempt to eliminate Decision Variable bounds that produce infeasible conditions.

Knapsack Example

Optimizing the Loading of a Limited Compartment

This is a classic Solver problem with many possible variations. Knapsack problems involve selecting the correct items to load into a compartment which is limited (Constrained) in some way such as by its size or maximum weight of its load. Objects selected for loading must maximize or minimize a given criterion while at the same time staying within the Constraints of the compartment.

These type of optimization problems are known as Knapsack Problems because of the well known classic example of selecting the correct items to optimally fill a camper's knapsack. The knapsack has a limited weight-carrying capacity and items are selected that optimize at least one criterion while not exceeding the knapsack's weight-carrying capacity.

The Problem

A knapsack is being loaded for a camping trip. This knapsack has a maximum weight-carrying limit and a maximum load size limit. The camper can choose from 4 different food items to put into the knapsack. The selected items must maximize the overall number calories and provide at least a minimum number of grams of protein while not exceeding the maximum load size and weight-carry capacity of the knapsack.

The knapsack's load cannot exceed a weight of 10 kilograms or a volume of 0.125 m³. The load of food items must contain at least 200 grams of protein.

The load may contain any number of each of the 4 following food items:

- **Candy Bar**
- **Sandwich**
- **Can of Juice**
- **Apple**

Specific information about each food items are as follows:

	Object	Calories Per Object	Protein (grams) Per Object	Weight (kg) Per Object	Volume (m^3) Per Object
34	Candy Bar	90	5	0.25	0.0005
35	Sandwich	130	40	0.35	0.002
36	Juice Can	100	15	0.35	0.00075
37	Apple	40	3	0.3	0.0009

Problem Solving Steps

Step 1 – Determine the Objective

In this case, the objective is to maximize the calories in the load. The cell calculating the sum total number of calories is the Objective Cell.

Step 2 – Determine the Decision Variables

We are trying to determine how many of each type of food object to carry in order to maximize the total number of calories while not exceeding the Constraints imposed on the problem. The Decision Variables are the numbers of each type of food item.

Step 3 – Build the Excel Equations That Combine the Objective With All Decision Variables

	A	B	C	D	E	F	G	H	I	J	K
1											
2		Object	Number of Objects	Calories		Protein (grams)		Weight of Object (kg)		Volume of Object (m^3)	
3				Per Object	Total	Per Object	Total	Per Object	Total	Per Object	Total
4		Candy Bar	5	90	450	5	25	0.25	1.25	0.0005	0.003
5		Sandwich	25	130	3250	40	1000	0.35	8.75	0.002	0.050
6		Juice Can	0	100	0	15	0	0.35	0	0.00075	0.000
7		Apple	0	40	0	3	0	0.3	0	0.0009	0.000
8		Column Totals	Decision Variables		Total Calories (Maximize)		Total Protein (g)		Total Weight (kg)		Total Volume (m^3)
9					3700		1025		10		0.0525
10					Objective		Constraint		Constraint		Constraint

The light gray Objective Cell, E7, displays the total number of calories and will be maximized. The dark gray Decision Variable cells (C4 to C7) display the number of each type of food item needed to achieve the objective.

Step 4 – List all Constraints

The medium gray Constraint cells in the model in the preceding image link to and are controlled by these medium gray user inputs in this following image.

	A	B	C	D	E	F	G
13		**Constraints**					
14							
15		10	=	Maximum Total Weight (kg)			
16							
17		0.125	=	Maximum Total Volume (m^3)			
18							
19		200	=	Minimum Total Protein (grams)			
20							
21							
22		Integer		All 4 Decision Variables (green cells)			
23				(Number of Candy Bars)			
24				(Number of Sandwiches)			
25				(Number of Juice Cans)			
26				(Number of Apples)			
27							
28							
29		Nonnegative		All Unconstrained Variables			

Step 5 – Test the Excel spreadsheet

Test the Excel spreadsheet completely before adding information to the Solver dialogue box. Make sure that any changes to Decision Variables produce the correct results in the Objective cell.

Step 6 – Insert All Data into the Solver Dialogue Box

Input the Objective cell, Decision Variable cell, and all Constraints into the Solver dialogue box as follows. Note that the Decision Variables (cells C4 to C7) are Constrained to having only integer values because only whole numbers of food objects can be carried. The other inequality Constraints link the user inputs to the model.

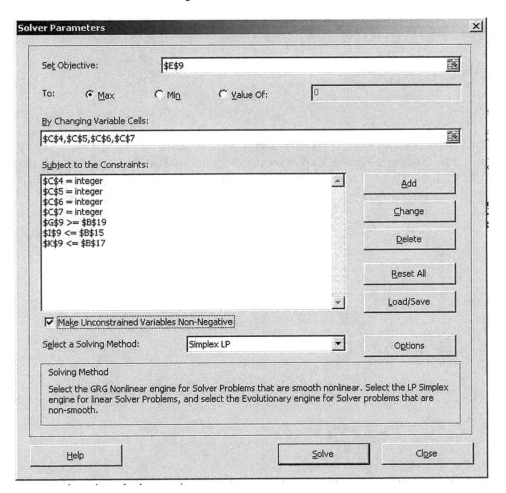

All equations on the Excel spreadsheet are linear (1st order) so we can use the Simplex LP (Linear Programming) Solver engine for this optimization problem.

Step 3 shows the completed problem with Decision Variables that have been optimized by the Solver to maximize the Objective while staying within the problem's Constraints.

Answer Report

Part 1

Note:
- The Solver Result
- How long Solver took to solve the problem
- The Solver Engine that was used and the Solver Options settings
- Where the Objective Cell was labeled in the Excel model for its name to appear as it does in Part 1 of the Answer Report

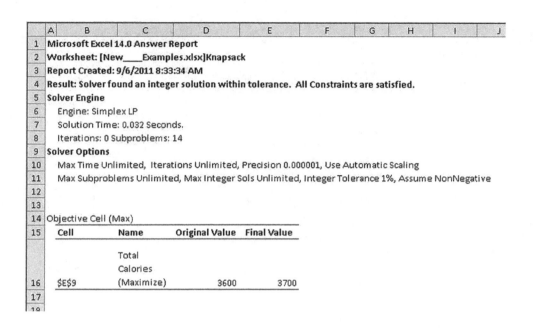

Part 2

- Note that the Variable Cells contain the Decision Variables
- Note where the labels for each Decision Variable are placed in the Excel model so that the Decision Variable's name will appear here in Part 2 of the Answer Report as it does
- Note the type of variable   - Either Continuous or Integer (**Integer**, Binary, or Alldifferent)
- Note the Before and After values of each Decision Variable

	A	B	C	D	E	F
19		Variable Cells				
20		Cell	Name	Original Value	Final Value	Integer
21		$C$4	Candy Bar Number of Objects	10	5	Integer
22		$C$5	Sandwich Number of Objects	10	25	Integer
23		$C$6	Juice Can Number of Objects	10	0	Integer
24		$C$7	Apple Number of Objects	10	0	Integer
25						

Part 3

- Note how each Constraint is labeled in the Excel model in order for the Constraint's name to appear here in Part 3 of the Answer Report as it does
- Note which Constraints are binding (had their limits hit) and which aren't.
- Note how much slack is still available in any Constraint that has not had its limit hit.
- Note any Integer Constraints (Integer, Binary, Alldifferent)

	Cell	Name	Cell Value	Formula	Status	Slack
27	Constraints					
28	Cell	Name	Cell Value	Formula	Status	Slack
29	$G$9	Total Protein (g)	1025	$G$9>=$B$19	Not Binding	825
30	$I$9	Total Weight (kg)	10	$I$9<=$B$15	Binding	0
31	$K$9	Total Volume (m3)	0.0525	$K$9<=$B$17	Not Binding	0.0725
32	$C$4=Integer					
33	$C$5=Integer					
34	$C$6=Integer					
35	$C$7=Integer					

Cutting Stock Example

Optimizing the Cutting of Strips of Sheet to Minimize Waste

This is another classic Solver problem with many possible variations. Cutting Stock problems involve cutting large sheets into the optimal number of smaller strips to meet customer orders while minimizing waste. The sheets can represent any type of material that come in a strip that is cut into smaller strips, such as a roll of steel. This problem involves rolls of garment that are cut to smaller sizes to meet individual customer orders.

The Problem

A garment factory produces rolls of garment in the following 2 sizes: rolls that are 75 inches wide and rolls that are 55 inches wide. Customers order garment rolls in the following 3 sizes: rolls that are 36 inches wide, rolls that are 25 inches wide, and rolls that are 13 inches wide.

The factory must cut the 75" rolls and 55" rolls in the correct number of 36", 25", and 13" rolls to meet individual customer orders while minimizing waste. Waste represents garment that is cut from the original 75" and 55" rolls which is not included in a customer order and is left-over.

Problem Solving Steps

Step 1 – Determine the Objective

In this case, the objective is to minimize the total waste left-over when satisfying each customer order. As seen in Step 3, Cutting Stock problems require listing all of the possible combinations that the original sheets can be cut in order to satisfy the customer's order.

The amount of waste (leftover material) from each combination is shown. The total amount of waste of all combinations that are cut is also listed. The objective is to determine the correct number of each combination to cut that will meet the customer's order and minimize the total amount of leftover, wasted garment. The Objective is to minimize the total amount of wasted garment. The cell is which the total waste from each order is calculated is the Objective Cell.

Step 2 – Determine the Decision Variables

We are trying to determine how many of each combination to cut that will satisfy the customer's order requirements and also minimize leftover wasted garment. The Decision Variables are the numbers of each type of cutting combination to cut.

Step 3 – Build the Excel Equations That Combine the Objective With All Decision Variables

The light gray Objective Cell, I16, displays the total amount of leftover garment that will be wasted when a specific group of cutting combinations is applied to meet a customer order. This will be minimized.

The dark gray Decision Variable cells, cells H4 to H14, display the number of each type of combination that will be cut to meet an individual customer order. Following is a complete view of the Excel model leading to the Objective.

	A	B	C	D	E	F	G	H	I
1									
2		Cutting Combination Number	Number of Final Cut Rolls Of Each Width Per Combination After Cutting			Garment Used When Cutting This Combo	Garment Leftover When Cutting This Combo	Number Cut	Total Waste From All Rolls Cut With This Combo
3			36"	25"	13"				
4		75" Combo 1	2	0	0	72	3	0	0
5		75" Combo 2	1	1	1	74	1	1	1
6		75" Combo 3	1	0	3	75	0	39	0
7		75" Combo 4	0	3	0	75	0	49	0
8		75" Combo 5	0	2	1	63	12	0	0
9		75" Combo 6	0	1	3	64	11	0	0
10		75" Combo 7	0	0	5	65	10	0	0
11		55" Combo 8	1	0	1	49	6	0	0
12		55" Combo 9	0	2	0	50	5	1	5
13		55" Combo 10	0	1	2	51	4	0	0
14		55" Combo 11	0	0	4	52	3	58	174
15								Decision Variables	Total Waste (Minimize)
16									180
17									Objective

The following 2 images present an expanded view for better clarity of the left and right halves of the preceding complete Excel model. The 1st image is the left side of the model and list all possible cutting combinations and the waste left-over from each. The 2nd image shown is the right side of the model with the dark gray Decision Variables and the light gray Objective Cell:

	A	B	C	D	E	F	G
1							
2		Cutting Combination Number	Number of Final Cut Rolls Of Each Width Per Combination After Cutting			Garment Used When Cutting This Combo	Garment Leftover When Cutting This Combo
3			36"	25"	13"		
4		75" Combo 1	2	0	0	72	3
5		75" Combo 2	1	1	1	74	1
6		75" Combo 3	1	0	3	75	0
7		75" Combo 4	0	3	0	75	0
8		75" Combo 5	0	2	1	63	12
9		75" Combo 6	0	1	3	64	11
10		75" Combo 7	0	0	5	65	10
11		55" Combo 8	1	0	1	49	6
12		55" Combo 9	0	2	0	50	5
13		55" Combo 10	0	1	2	51	4
14		55" Combo 11	0	0	4	52	3

	F	G	H	I
1				
2	Garment Used When Cutting This Combo	Garment Leftover When Cutting This Combo	Number Cut	Total Waste From All Rolls Cut With This Combo
3				
4	72	3	0	0
5	74	1	1	1
6	75	0	39	0
7	75	0	49	0
8	63	12	0	0
9	64	11	0	0
10	65	10	0	0
11	49	6	0	0
12	50	5	1	5
13	51	4	0	0
14	52	3	58	174
15			Decision Variables	Total Waste (Minimize)
16				180
17				Objective

Step 4 – List all Constraints

	36"	25"	13"	Number of Initial Rolls Cut With This Combo	36"	25"	13"
	Number of Final Cut Rolls Of Each Width Per Combination After Cutting				Total Number of Final Cut Rolls Of Each Width After Cutting		
23	36"	25"	13"		36"	25"	13"
24	2	0	0	0	0	0	0
25	1	1	1	1	1	1	1
26	1	0	3	39	39	0	117
27	0	3	0	49	0	147	0
28	0	2	1	0	0	0	0
29	0	1	3	0	0	0	0
30	0	0	5	0	0	0	0
31	1	0	1	0	0	0	0
32	0	2	0	1	0	2	0
33	0	1	2	0	0	0	0
34	0	0	4	58	0	0	232
35					Total Number of 36" Rolls Cut	Total Number of 25" Rolls Cut	Total Number of 13" Rolls Cut
36	Column Totals				40	150	350
					Constraint	Constraint	Constraint

The medium gray Constraint cells in the model the preceding image link to the medium gray user-controlled inputs outside of the model in the following image. The user-controlled inputs represent the customer's order as follows:

	B	C	D	E	F	G	H	I
38		Constraints						
39		40	=	Total Number of 36" Rolls Ordered (Equals Number of 36" Rolls Cut)				
40								
41		150	=	Total Number of 25" Rolls Ordered (Equals Number of 25" Rolls Cut)				
42								
43		350	=	Total Number of 13" Rolls Ordered (Equals Number of 13" Rolls Cut)				
44								
45								
46								
47		Integer		All 11 Decision Variables (green cells)				
48				(Number of Initial Rolls Cut with Each Combo)				
49								
50								
51		Nonnegative		All Unconstrained Variables				

Step 5 – Test the Excel spreadsheet

Test the Excel spreadsheet completely before adding information to the Solver dialogue box. Make sure that any changes to Decision Variables produce the correct results in the Objective cell.

Step 6 – Insert All Data into the Solver Dialogue Box

Input the Objective cell, Decision Variable cell, and all Constraints into the Solver dialogue box as follows:

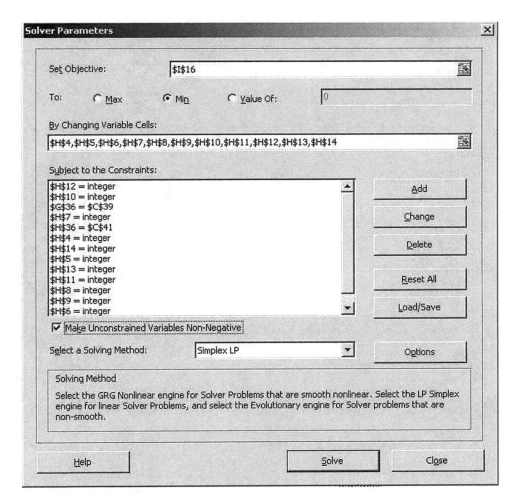

Note that the Decision Variables are Constrained to be integers because only whole numbers of garment rolls can be cut. The equality Constraints are the links between the number of garment rolls in the customer's order and the model. Unconstrained variables are made nonnegative to ensure that there can be no negative numbers of rolls cut.

There are still a few more Constraints not shown in the preceding image that are shown as follows by scrolling down the slider bar next to the Constraints:

All equations on the Excel spreadsheet are linear (1st order) so we can use the Simplex LP (Linear Programming) Solver engine for this optimization problem.

Step 3 shows the completed problem with Decision Variables that have been optimized by the Solver to maximize the Objective while staying within the problem's Constraints.

Answer Report

Part 1

Note:
- The Solver Result
- How long Solver took to solve the problem
- The Solver Engine that was used and the Solver Options settings
- Where the Objective Cell was labeled in the Excel model for its name to appear as it does in Part 1 of the Answer Report

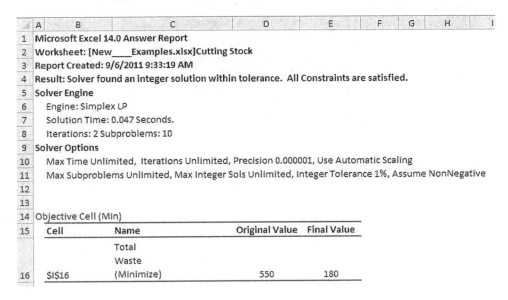

	A	B	C	D	E	F	G	H	I
1	Microsoft Excel 14.0 Answer Report								
2	Worksheet: [New___Examples.xlsx]Cutting Stock								
3	Report Created: 9/6/2011 9:33:19 AM								
4	Result: Solver found an integer solution within tolerance. All Constraints are satisfied.								
5	Solver Engine								
6	Engine: Simplex LP								
7	Solution Time: 0.047 Seconds.								
8	Iterations: 2 Subproblems: 10								
9	Solver Options								
10	Max Time Unlimited, Iterations Unlimited, Precision 0.000001, Use Automatic Scaling								
11	Max Subproblems Unlimited, Max Integer Sols Unlimited, Integer Tolerance 1%, Assume NonNegative								
12									
13									
14	Objective Cell (Min)								
15	Cell	Name		Original Value	Final Value				
16	$I$16	Total Waste (Minimize)		550	180				

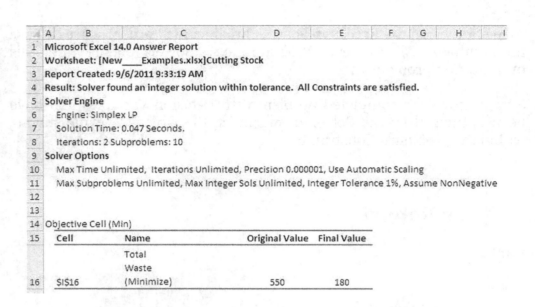

▲	A	B	C	D	E	F	G	H	I
1	Microsoft Excel 14.0 Answer Report								
2	Worksheet: [New____Examples.xlsx]Cutting Stock								
3	Report Created: 9/6/2011 9:33:19 AM								
4	Result: Solver found an integer solution within tolerance. All Constraints are satisfied.								
5	Solver Engine								
6	Engine: Simplex LP								
7	Solution Time: 0.047 Seconds.								
8	Iterations: 2 Subproblems: 10								
9	Solver Options								
10	Max Time Unlimited, Iterations Unlimited, Precision 0.000001, Use Automatic Scaling								
11	Max Subproblems Unlimited, Max Integer Sols Unlimited, Integer Tolerance 1%, Assume NonNegative								
12									
13									
14	Objective Cell (Min)								
15	Cell	Name		Original Value	Final Value				
16	$I$16	Total Waste (Minimize)		550	180				

Part 2

- Note that the Variable Cells contain the Decision Variables
- Note where the labels for each Decision Variable are placed in the Excel model so that the Decision Variable's name will appear here in Part 2 of the Answer Report as it does
- Note the type of variable   - Either Continuous or Integer (**Integer**, Binary, or Alldifferent)
- Note the Before and After values of each Decision Variable

	Cell	Name	Original Value	Final Value	Integer
19	Variable Cells				
20	Cell	Name	Original Value	Final Value	Integer
21	$H$4	75" Combo 1 Number Cut	10	0	Integer
22	$H$5	75" Combo 2 Number Cut	10	1	Integer
23	$H$6	75" Combo 3 Number Cut	10	39	Integer
24	$H$7	75" Combo 4 Number Cut	10	49	Integer
25	$H$8	75" Combo 5 Number Cut	10	0	Integer
26	$H$9	75" Combo 6 Number Cut	10	0	Integer
27	$H$10	75" Combo 7 Number Cut	10	0	Integer
28	$H$11	55" Combo 8 Number Cut	10	0	Integer
29	$H$12	55" Combo 9 Number Cut	10	1	Integer
30	$H$13	55" Combo 10 Number Cut	10	0	Integer
31	$H$14	55" Combo 11 Number Cut	10	58	Integer

Part 3

- Note how each Constraint is labeled in the Excel model in order for the Constraint's name to appear here in Part 3 of the Answer Report as it does
- Note which Constraints are binding (had their limits hit) and which aren't.
- Note how much slack is still available in any Constraint that has not had its limit hit.
- Note any Integer Constraints (Integer, Binary, Alldifferent)

	Cell	Name	Cell Value	Formula	Status	Slack
33						
34	Constraints					
35	Cell	Name	Cell Value	Formula	Status	Slack
36	$I$36	Total Number of 13" Rolls Cut	350	$I$36=$C$43	Binding	0
37	$H$36	Total Number of 25" Rolls Cut	150	$H$36=$C$41	Binding	0
38	$G$36	Total Number of 36" Rolls Cut	40	$G$36=$C$39	Binding	0
39	$H$7=Integer					
40	$H$11=Integer					
41	$H$6=Integer					
42	$H$8=Integer					
43	$H$9=Integer					
44	$H$14=Integer					
45	$H$5=Integer					
46	$H$4=Integer					
47	$H$13=Integer					
48	$H$12=Integer					
49	$H$10=Integer					

Machine Selection Example

Selecting Machines to Optimally Fulfill an Order

This Solver problem involves dividing a task among different machines to fulfill a customer order while minimizing total cost. Each machine varies in operating cost, production speed, and ability to perform different elements of the task. The correct combination of machines must be selected to fulfill individual customer orders and minimize the total cost of order fulfillment.

The Problem

3 machines perform the same generic type of task; they all make bolts. Each machine varies in the variety of bolts that it can produce. Each machine also has a different operating cost and a different operating speed. The objective is to fulfill an individual customer order within a specified time limit while minimizing the total cost of fulfilling this order.

500 minutes is the total time allowed to complete this entire order.

Shown as follows are the specific details about each machine:

		Speed	Operating Cost Per Output Unit	Levels of Capability		
		Number of Bolts Per Minute	Operating Cost per 100 Bolts Produced	Ability To Make 1" Bolts	Ability To Make 2" Bolts	Ability To Make 3" Bolts
	Machine 1	5	$25	1	1	1
	Machine 2	9	$14	1	1	0
	Machine 3	25	$4	1	0	0

Problem Solving Steps

Step 1 – Determine the Objective

In this case, the objective is to minimize the total cost of operating the machines while fulfilling the customer's order within the specified time limit. The cell which calculates this total cost is the Objective Cell.

Step 2 – Determine the Decision Variables

An individual customer order is simply a request to make a certain number of each of the 3 available bolts (1 inch bolts, 3 inch bolts, and 3 inch bolts). There are 3 machine available to fulfill this order. We must determine how many bolts of each type to produce on each machine in order to fulfill the order within the given time frame and at the lowest total cost. The Decision Variables are numbers of each type of bolt that each machine will produce.

Step 3 – Build the Excel Equations That Combine the Objective With All Decision Variables

	A	B	C	D	E	F	G	H
9								
10			Bolts Produced (Decision Variables)			Number of Bolts	Cost Per 100 Bolts	Total Cost
11			1" Bolts Cut	2" Bolts Cut	3" Bolts Cut	Per Machine	Per Machine	Per Machine
12		Machine 1	0	2000	400	2400	$25	$600
13		Machine 2	3500	1000		4500	$14	$630
14		Machine 3	12500			12500	$4	$500
15								Total Cost (Minimize)
16								$1,730
								Objective

The light gray Objective Cell, H16, displays the total cost of fulfilling the order using all 3 machines. This will be minimized. The dark gray Decision Variable cells (C12, C13, C14, D12, D13, E12) display the numbers of each type of bolt that each machine will produce.

Step 4 – List all Constraints

	A	B	C	D	E	F	G	H
19		**Constraints**						
20								
21								
22			Bolts Produced			Number of Bolts Per Machine	Number of Bolts Per Minute	Total Minutes Per Machine
23			1"	2"	3"			
24		Machine 1	0	2000	400	2400	5	480
25		Machine 2	3500	1000		4500	9	500
26		Machine 3	12500			12500	25	500
			Total Number 1" Bolts In Order	Total Number 2" Bolts In Order	Total Number 3" Bolts In Order			Constraints
27								
28			16000	3000	400			
29			Constraint	Constraint	Constraint			

The medium gray Constraint cells in the model in the preceding image link to the medium gray user inputs in the following image.

	A	B	C	D	E	F	G
30							
31		Constraints					
32		16000	=	Total Number of 1" Bolts in Order			
33							
34		3000	=	Total Number of 2" Bolts in Order			
35							
36		400	=	Total Number of 3" Bolts in Order			
37							
38							
39		500	=	Maximum Time Allowed For Order (Minutes)			
40							
41							
42		Integer		All 6 Decision Variables (green cells)			
43				(Number of bolts produced per machine)			
44							
45		Nonnegative		All Unconstrained Variables			

The medium gray user-input cells (B32, B34, B36) represent the customer's order. The number of bolts produced by each machine (the Decision Variables) must be whole numbers (integers) and cannot be negative.

Step 5 – Test the Excel spreadsheet

Test the Excel spreadsheet completely before adding information to the Solver dialogue box. Make sure that any changes to Decision Variables produce the correct results in the Objective cell.

Step 6 – Insert All Data into the Solver Dialogue Box

Input the Objective cell, Decision Variable cell, and all Constraints into the Solver dialogue box as follows:

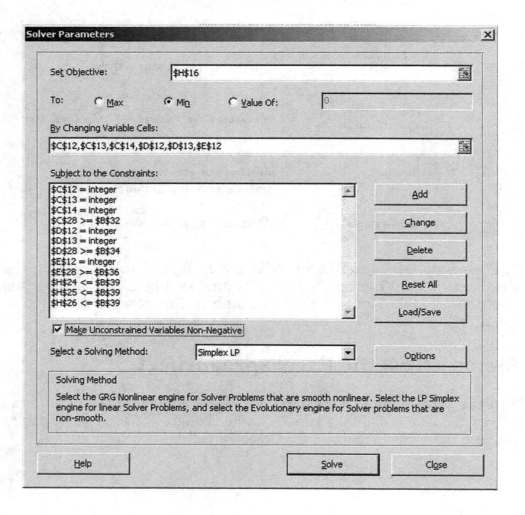

The number of bolts produced by each machine (the Decision Variables)

must be whole numbers (integers) and cannot be negative.

All equations on the Excel spreadsheet are linear (1st order) so we can use the Simplex LP (Linear Programming) Solver engine for this optimization problem.

Step 3 shows the completed problem with Decision Variables that have been optimized by the Solver to maximize the Objective while staying within the problem's Constraints.

Answer Report

Part 1

Note:
- The Solver Result
- How long Solver took to solve the problem
- The Solver Engine that was used and the Solver Options settings
- Where the Objective Cell was labeled in the Excel model for its name to appear as it does in Part 1 of the Answer Report

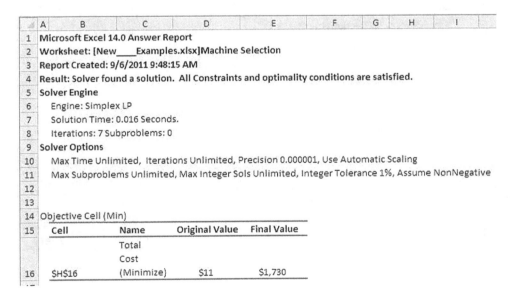

	A	B	C	D	E	F	G	H	I
1	Microsoft Excel 14.0 Answer Report								
2	Worksheet: [New____Examples.xlsx]Machine Selection								
3	Report Created: 9/6/2011 9:48:15 AM								
4	Result: Solver found a solution. All Constraints and optimality conditions are satisfied.								
5	Solver Engine								
6	Engine: Simplex LP								
7	Solution Time: 0.016 Seconds.								
8	Iterations: 7 Subproblems: 0								
9	Solver Options								
10	Max Time Unlimited, Iterations Unlimited, Precision 0.000001, Use Automatic Scaling								
11	Max Subproblems Unlimited, Max Integer Sols Unlimited, Integer Tolerance 1%, Assume NonNegative								
12									
13									
14	Objective Cell (Min)								
15		Cell	Name	Original Value	Final Value				
16	$H$16	Total Cost (Minimize)	$11	$1,730					

Part 2

- Note that the Variable Cells contain the Decision Variables
- Note where the labels for each Decision Variable are placed in the Excel model so that the Decision Variable's name will appear here in Part 2 of the Answer Report as it does
- Note the type of variable - Either Continuous or Integer (**Integer**, Binary, or Alldifferent)
- Note the Before and After values of each Decision Variable

	A	B	C	D	E	F
19	Variable Cells					
20		Cell	Name	Original Value	Final Value	Integer
21		$C$12	Machine 1 1" Bolts Cut	10	0	Integer
22		$C$13	Machine 2 1" Bolts Cut	10	3500	Integer
23		$C$14	Machine 3 1" Bolts Cut	10	12500	Integer
24		$D$12	Machine 1 2" Bolts Cut	10	2000	Integer
25		$D$13	Machine 2 2" Bolts Cut	10	1000	Integer
26		$E$12	Machine 1 3" Bolts Cut	10	400	Integer

Part 3

- Note how each Constraint is labeled in the Excel model in order for the Constraint's name to appear here in Part 3 of the Answer Report as it does
- Note which Constraints are binding (had their limits hit) and which aren't.
- Note how much slack is still available in any Constraint that has not had its limit hit.
- Note any Integer Constraints (Integer, Binary, Alldifferent)

	A	B	C	D	E	F	G
27							
28							
29	Constraints						
30		Cell	Name	Cell Value	Formula	Status	Slack
31		$C$28	Total Number 1" Bolts In Order	16000	$C$28>=$B$32	Binding	0
32		$D$28	Total Number 2" Bolts In Order	3000	$D$28>=$B$34	Binding	0
33		$E$28	Total Number 3" Bolts In Order	400	$E$28>=$B$36	Binding	0
34		$H$24	Machine 1 Total Minutes Per Machine	480	$H$24<=$B$39	Not Binding	20
35		$H$25	Machine 2 Total Minutes Per Machine	500	$H$25<=$B$39	Binding	0

	B	C	D	E	F	G
35	$H$25	Machine 2 Total Minutes Per Machine	500	$H$25<=$B$39	Binding	0
36	$H$26	Machine 3 Total Minutes Per Machine	500	$H$26<=$B$39	Binding	0
37	$C$12=Integer					
38	$C$13=Integer					
39	$C$14=Integer					
40	$D$12=Integer					
41	$D$13=Integer					
42	$E$12=Integer					

Maximizing Employee Satisfaction Example

Optimal Assignment of Company Assets Among Employees For Maximum Satisfaction

In this problem the Solver is used to determine how to assign similar company assets among employees to produce maximum overall satisfaction. Generically this problem can be used to determine how to optimally divide up a group of similar objects among a group of people.

Each person in the group is surveyed to determine how desirable they rate each object to be distributed. In this case, 4 sales territories will be assigned among 4 salespeople. The Excel Solver will select the single, unique territory to be assigned to each salesperson in order to maximize cumulative satisfaction among all 4 people.

The Problem

4 sales territories will be assigned to 4 salespeople. Each salesperson will be assigned to a separate territory. Each salesperson is surveyed to determine his or her liking for each of the 4 sales territories. Each salesperson will rate the desirability of each sales territory on a scale of 1 to 5. A score is 5 is the highest and indicates that the salesperson favors this territory above the other 3. The salespeople are required to assign a different rating to each of the 4 territories.

Individual ratings from each salesperson are as follows:

	A	B	C	D	E	F
1						
2			Sales Territory 1	Sales Territory 2	Sales Territory 3	Sales Territory 4
3		Salesperson 1	1	3	5	4
4		Salesperson 2	4	1	5	3
5		Salesperson 3	5	2	4	3
6		Salesperson 4	4	1	2	5
7						

A rating of 5 indicates maximum desirability. The lowest desirability rating is a 1.

Use this information to determine the optimal assignment of sales territories among the salespeople that will maximize cumulative satisfaction among the entire sales force.

Problem Solving Steps

Step 1 – Determine the Objective

In this case, the objective is to maximize cumulative satisfaction among the 4 salespeople. The Objective cell will contain the sum of the satisfaction ratings that each salesperson had previously rated his or her newly-assigned territory.

Step 2 – Determine the Decision Variables

We are trying to determine which territory to assign to each salesperson in order to maximize cumulative satisfaction. The Decision Variables will be binary variables having the values of only 1 or 0, which will indicate whether or not a specific sales territory will be assigned to specific salesperson.

The Decision Variables will be forced to be binary by using numerical Constraints, not the built-in Binary Integer Constraint.

Step 3 – Build the Excel Equations That Combine the Objective and Decision Variables

	A	B	C	D	E	F	G
11			Decision Variables (Can Only Be Either 1 or 0) (Made To Be Binary By Setting Columns Totals To 1)				
12							
13			In Territory 1 ?	In Territory 2 ?	InTerritory 3 ?	In Territory 4 ?	Total Number of Territories Assigned To This Salesperson
14		Salesperson 1	0	1	0	0	1
15		Salesperson 2	0	0	1	0	1
16		Salesperson 3	1	0	0	0	1
17		Salesperson 4	0	0	0	1	1
							Constraints
18			Total Number Salespeople In Territory 1	Total Number Salespeople In Territory 2	Total Number Salespeople In Territory 3	Total Number Salespeople In Territory 4	
19			1	1	1	1	
20			Constraint	Constraint	Constraint	Constraint	

C25 ▼ fx =IF(C14=1,C5," ")

	A	B	C	D	E	F	G
21							
22		If-Then-Else	Cell C25 Contains: =IF(C14=1,C5," ")				
23			All Cells From C23 to G26 Have Similar If-Then-Else Statements				
24			Sales Territory 1	Sales Territory 2	Sales Territory 3	Sales Territory 4	Satisfaction With Final Choices
25		Salesperson 1		3			3
26		Salesperson 2			5		5
27		Salesperson 3	5				5
28		Salesperson 4				5	5
29							Cumulative Satisfaction With Final Choices (Maximize)
30							18
31							Objective

Note that the dark gray Decision Variables (cells C14 to F17) were forced to be binary by Constraining their row totals (medium gray cells G14 to G17) and column totals (medium gray cells C19 to F19) to 1. We did not in this apply the built-in Binary Integer Constraint because of this.

How To Display Only the Satisfaction Rating Associated With Each Salesperson's Assigned Territory

Note the If-Then-Else statements in each of the cells in the preceding image.

As shown above, Cell C25 contains: **=IF(C14=1,C5, " ")**. This If-Then-Else statement translates to: If Cell C14 contains "1," then copy the contents of Cell C5 into Cell C25, else leave Cell C25 blank.

In this case, the If-Then-Else statements place the salesperson's desirability rating of that territory (Cell C5) into Cell C25 only if Solver has assigned that territory to the salesperson (if Solver has assigned a "1" in Cell C14).

If-Then-Else statements are some of the most useful tools in Excel. If you create Excel models often, you should definitely master the If-Then-Else statement.

The light gray Objective cell displays the combined level of employee satisfaction and will be maximized. The Decision Variable cells are binary and display whether or not the particular territory will be assign the respective salesperson.

Step 4 – List all Constraints

	A	B	C	D	E	F
32						
33		Constraints				
34		1	=	Total Number of Salespeople in Territory 1		
35						
36		1	=	Total Number of Salespeople in Territory 2		
37						
38		1	=	Total Number of Salespeople in Territory 3		
39						
40		1	=	Total Number of Salespeople in Territory 4		
41						
42						
43		1	=	Total Number of Territories For Each Salesperson		
44						
45						
46		Integer		All 12 Decision Variables (green cells)		
47				(Satisfaction Survey Scores)		
48						
49		Nonnegative		All Unconstrained Variables		

Once again note that no Binary Constraint was used because the Decision Variables were forced to be binary by setting row and column totals to 1 using the Constraints in the preceding image.

These Constraints could be varied to allow more than 1 salesperson to be assigned to any of the territories, or allow each salesperson to be assigned more than 1 territory. Try varying the Constraints on the downloadable Excel workbook containing this and all other examples in this manual.

Step 5 – Test the Excel spreadsheet

Test the Excel spreadsheet completely before adding information to the Solver dialogue box. Make sure that any changes to Decision Variables produce the correct results in the Objective cell.

Step 6 – Insert All Data into the Solver Dialogue Box

Input the Objective cell, Decision Variable cell, and all Constraints into the Solver dialogue box as follows:

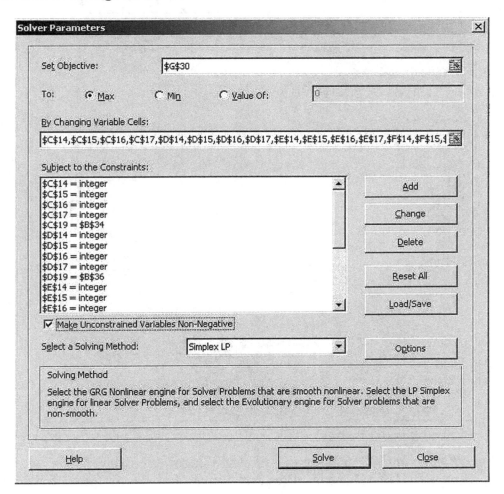

The Integer Constraints ensure that only a whole number of salespeople occupy each territory. The equality Constraints ensure that every salesperson gets assigned 1 unique territory. These equality Constraints also ensure that the Decision Variables are binary.

If we scroll down the Constraints, we can see the rest of the Constraints as follows:

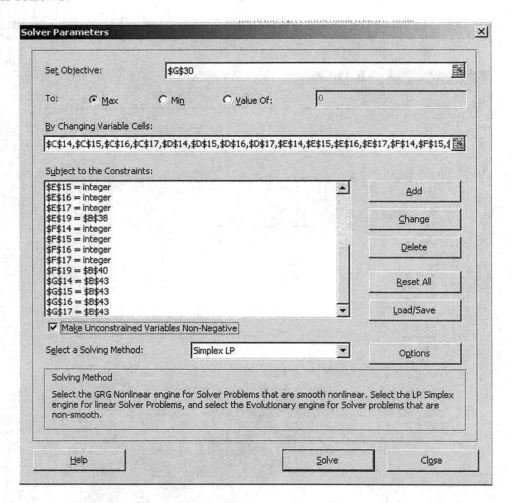

All equations on the Excel spreadsheet are linear (1st order) so we can use the Simplex LP (Linear Programming) Solver engine for this optimization problem.

Step 3 shows the completed problem with Decision Variables that have been optimized by the Solver to maximize the Objective while staying within the problem's Constraints.

Answer Report

Part 1

Note:
- The Solver Result
- How long Solver took to solve the problem
- The Solver Engine that was used and the Solver Options settings
- Where the Objective Cell was labeled in the Excel model for its name to appear as it does in Part 1 of the Answer Report

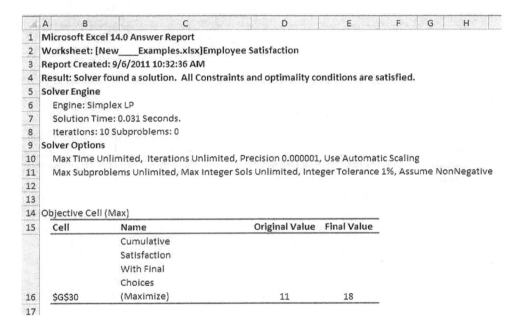

	A	B	C	D	E	F	G	H
1	Microsoft Excel 14.0 Answer Report							
2	Worksheet: [New____Examples.xlsx]Employee Satisfaction							
3	Report Created: 9/6/2011 10:32:36 AM							
4	Result: Solver found a solution. All Constraints and optimality conditions are satisfied.							
5	Solver Engine							
6	Engine: Simplex LP							
7	Solution Time: 0.031 Seconds.							
8	Iterations: 10 Subproblems: 0							
9	Solver Options							
10	Max Time Unlimited, Iterations Unlimited, Precision 0.000001, Use Automatic Scaling							
11	Max Subproblems Unlimited, Max Integer Sols Unlimited, Integer Tolerance 1%, Assume NonNegative							
12								
13								
14	Objective Cell (Max)							
15		Cell	Name	Original Value	Final Value			
16		$G$30	Cumulative Satisfaction With Final Choices (Maximize)	11	18			
17								

Part 2

- Note that the Variable Cells contain the Decision Variables
- Note where the labels for each Decision Variable are placed in the Excel model so that the Decision Variable's name will appear here in Part 2 of the Answer Report as it does
- Note the type of variable   - Either Continuous or Integer (**Integer**, Binary, or Alldifferent)
- Note the Before and After values of each Decision Variable

	A	B	C	D	E	F
19	Variable Cells					
20		Cell	Name	Original Value	Final Value	Integer
21		$C$14	Salesperson 1 In Territory 1 ?	1	0	Integer
22		$C$15	Salesperson 2 In Territory 1 ?	0	0	Integer
23		$C$16	Salesperson 3 In Territory 1 ?	0	1	Integer
24		$C$17	Salesperson 4 In Territory 1 ?	0	0	Integer
25		$D$14	Salesperson 1 In Territory 2 ?	0	1	Integer
26		$D$15	Salesperson 2 In Territory 2 ?	1	0	Integer
27		$D$16	Salesperson 3 In Territory 2 ?	0	0	Integer
28		$D$17	Salesperson 4 In Territory 2 ?	0	0	Integer
29		$E$14	Salesperson 1 InTerritory 3 ?	0	0	Integer
30		$E$15	Salesperson 2 InTerritory 3 ?	0	1	Integer
31		$E$16	Salesperson 3 InTerritory 3 ?	1	0	Integer
32		$E$17	Salesperson 4 InTerritory 3 ?	0	0	Integer
33		$F$14	Salesperson 1 In Territory 4 ?	0	0	Integer
34		$F$15	Salesperson 2 In Territory 4 ?	0	0	Integer
35		$F$16	Salesperson 3 In Territory 4 ?	0	0	Integer
36		$F$17	Salesperson 4 In Territory 4 ?	1	1	Integer
37						

Part 3

- Note how each Constraint is labeled in the Excel model in order for the Constraint's name to appear here in Part 3 of the Answer Report as it does
- Note which Constraints are binding (had their limits hit) and which aren't.
- Note how much slack is still available in any Constraint that has not had its limit hit.
- Note any Integer Constraints (Integer, Binary, Alldifferent)

	A	B	C	D	E	F	G
37							
38							
39	Constraints						
40		Cell	Name	Cell Value	Formula	Status	Slack
41		$C$19	Total Number Salespeople In Territory 1	1	$C$19=$B$34	Binding	0
42		$D$19	Total Number Salespeople In Territory 2	1	$D$19=$B$36	Binding	0
43		$E$19	Total Number Salespeople In Territory 3	1	$E$19=$B$38	Binding	0
44		$F$19	Total Number Salespeople In Territory 4	1	$F$19=$B$40	Binding	0
45		$G$14	Salesperson 1 Total Number of Territories Assigned To This Salesperson	1	$G$14=$B$43	Binding	0

	A	B	C	D	E	F	G
45		$G$14	Salesperson 1 Total Number of Territories Assigned To This Salesperson	1	$G$14=$B$43	Binding	0
46		$G$15	Salesperson 2 Total Number of Territories Assigned To This Salesperson	1	$G$15=$B$43	Binding	0
47		$G$16	Salesperson 3 Total Number of Territories Assigned To This Salesperson	1	$G$16=$B$43	Binding	0
48		$G$17	Salesperson 4 Total Number of Territories Assigned To This Salesperson	1	$G$17=$B$43	Binding	0

	A	B	C	D	E	F	G
48		$G$17	Salesperson 4 Total Number of Territories Assigned To This Salesperson	1	$G$17=$B$43	Binding	0
49		$C$14=Integer					
50		$C$15=Integer					
51		$C$16=Integer					
52		$C$17=Integer					
53		$D$14=Integer					
54		$D$15=Integer					
55		$D$16=Integer					
56		$D$17=Integer					
57		$E$14=Integer					
58		$E$15=Integer					
59		$E$16=Integer					
60		$E$17=Integer					
61		$F$14=Integer					
62		$F$15=Integer					
63		$F$16=Integer					
64		$F$17=Integer					

Shipping Cost Minimization Example

Minimizing the Total Cost of Shipping From Multiple Points To Multiple Points

This Solver problem minimizes the total cost of shipping the same product from multiple factories to multiple stores. Shipping costs are different from each factory to each store. Each store needs a different quantity of the product and each factory has a different amount of the product available for shipping. This problem assumes that the only cost differences are the per unit shipping costs between the factories and the stores.

The Problem

A company manufactures its own products at its 3 factories and then delivers these products at its own 3 stores. Each of the 3 stores orders a different amount of the product from the factories while each of the 3 factories has a different amount of the product available to ship to the stores. Shipping costs per unit of product are different between each factory and each store. Determine the optimal amount of product to ship from each factory to each store in order to minimize total shipping costs while fulfilling each store's order.

Shown as follows are the costs of shipping a single unit of the product from each factory to each store :

	A	B	C	D	E
1					
2		Shipping Cost Per Unit			
3					
4			Store 1	Store 2	Store 3
5		Factory 1	$4	$1	$7
6		Factory 2	$6	$2	$2
7		Factory 3	$3	$4	$3

Problem Solving Steps

Step 1 – Determine the Objective

In this case, the objective is to minimize the total cost of shipping between all factories and all stores. The cell in which that total cost is calculated is the Objective Cell.

Step 2 – Determine the Decision Variables

We are trying to determine how many units of product to ship from each factory to each store in order to minimize total shipping cost while fulfilling all store orders. The Decision Variables are the numbers of units of the product to ship from each factory to each store.

Step 3 – Build the Excel Equations That Combine the Objective With All Decision Variables

	A	B	C	D	E	F	G	H	I	J	K	L	M
9													
10				Store 1		Store 2		Store 3					
11			(Decision Variables)		(Decision Variables)		(Decision Variables)						
12			Number of Units Shipped To Store 1	Total Cost of Shipping To Store 1	Number of Units Shipped To Store 2	Total Cost of Shipping To Store 2	Number of Units Shipped To Store 3	Total Cost of Shipping To Store 3		Total Units Shipped			
13		Factory 1	20	$80	40	$40	0	$0		60	= Units Shipped from Factory 1		
14		Factory 2	0	$0	0	$0	200	$400		200	= Units Shipped from Factory 2		
15		Factory 3	90	$270	0	$0	40	$120		130	= Units Shipped from Factory 3		
										Constraints			
16			Total Number of Units Shipped To Store 1	Total Cost of Shipping To Store 1	Total Number of Units Shipped To Store 2	Total Cost of Shipping To Store 2	Total Number of Units Shipped To Store 3	Total Cost of Shipping To Store 3					
17			110	$350	40	$40	240	$520					
18			Constraint		Constraint		Constraint						
19				Total Cost of Shipping (Minimize)									
20				$910									
21				Objective									

The preceding image of the model shows the light gray Objective cell (D20), the dark gray Decision Variables (C13 to C15, E13 to E15, G13 to G15), and the medium gray Constraint cells (C17, E17, G17, J13 to J15).

Following on the next several pages is an expanded view of this Excel model for greater clarity.

The next image shows a close-up of the part of the model containing all the dark gray Decision Variables and the medium gray Constraint cells that Constraint the amount shipped to each store.

	A	B	C	D	E	F	G	H
9								
10			Store 1		Store 2		Store 3	
11			(Decision Variables)		(Decision Variables)		(Decision Variables)	
12			Number of Units Shipped To Store 1	Total Cost of Shipping To Store 1	Number of Units Shipped To Store 2	Total Cost of Shipping To Store 2	Number of Units Shipped To Store 3	Total Cost of Shipping To Store 3
13		Factory 1	20	$80	40	$40	0	$0
14		Factory 2	0	$0	0	$0	200	$400
15		Factory 3	90	$270	0	$0	40	$120
16			Total Number of Units Shipped To Store 1	Total Cost of Shipping To Store 1	Total Number of Units Shipped To Store 2	Total Cost of Shipping To Store 2	Total Number of Units Shipped To Store 3	Total Cost of Shipping To Store 3
17			110	$350	40	$40	240	$520
18			Constraint		Constraint		Constraint	

Following are the light gray Objective total cost of shipping and the medium gray Constraint cells that ensure that each store will receive its required number of units of product.

	B	C	D	E	F	G	H
16		Total Number of Units Shipped To Store 1	Total Cost of Shipping To Store 1	Total Number of Units Shipped To Store 2	Total Cost of Shipping To Store 2	Total Number of Units Shipped To Store 3	Total Cost of Shipping To Store 3
17		110	$350	40	$40	240	$520
18		Constraint		Constraint		Constraint	
19			Total Cost of Shipping (Minimize)				
20			$910				
21			Objective				

Following are the medium gray Constraint cells that ensure that each factory will not attempt to ship more units than that factory has available.

	I	J	K	L	M
12		Total Units Shipped			
13		60	= Units Shipped from Factory 1		
14		200	= Units Shipped from Factory 2		
15		130	= Units Shipped from Factory 3		
		Constraints			

Step 4 – List all Constraints

	A	B	C	D	E	F	G	H
22		**Constraints**						
23								
24		100	= Units Available from Factory 1			≥ Units Shipped from Factory 1		
25		200	= Units Available from Factory 2			≥ Units Shipped from Factory 2		
26		130	= Units Available from Factory 3			≥ Units Shipped from Factory 3		
27								
28		110	= Total Number of Units Ordered By Store 1					
29		40	= Total Number of Units Ordered By Store 2					
30		240	= Total Number of Units Ordered By Store 3					
31								
32								
33								
34		Integer		All 9 Decision Variables (green cells)				
35				(Number of Units Shipped To Each Store From Each Factory)				
36								
37		Nonnegative		All Unconstrained Variables				

The medium gray Constraint cells shown here are the cells on the spreadsheet where the user inputs the number of units of product needed from each store and the number available from each factory.

Step 5 – Test the Excel spreadsheet

Test the Excel spreadsheet completely before adding information to the Solver dialogue box. Make sure that any changes to Decision Variables produce the correct results in the Objective cell.

Step 6 – Insert All Data into the Solver Dialogue Box

Input the Objective cell, Decision Variable cell, and all Constraints into the Solver dialogue box as follows:

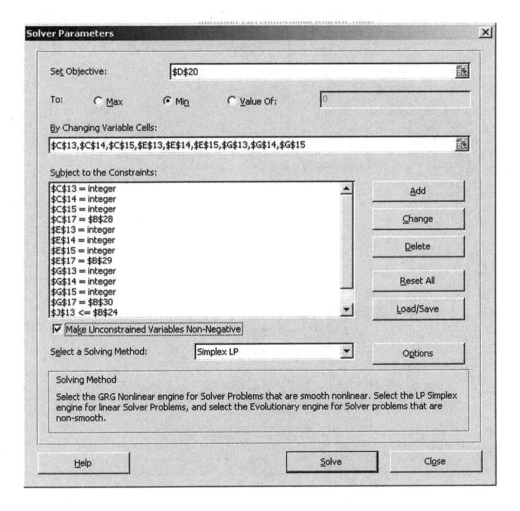

The Integer Constraints ensure that only whole number of units of product get shipped. The equality Constraints ensure that each store's order will be exactly fulfilled. The inequality Constraints ensure that no factory attempts to ship more product than it has available.

We have to scroll down to view the remaining Constraints, as follows:

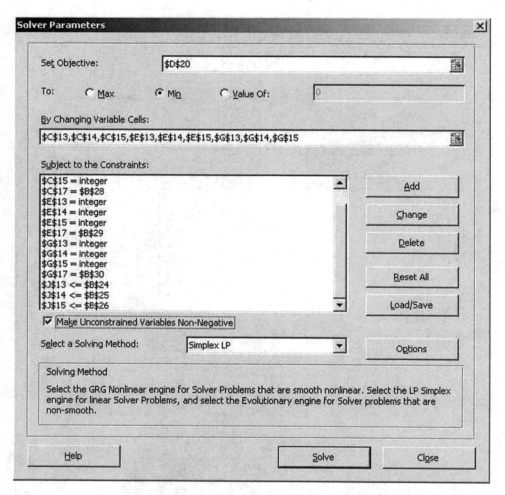

All equations on the Excel spreadsheet are linear (1st order) so we can use the Simplex LP (Linear Programming) Solver engine for this optimization problem.

Step 3 shows the completed problem with Decision Variables that have been optimized by the Solver to maximize the Objective while staying within the problem's Constraints.

Answer Report

Part 1

Note:
- The Solver Result
- How long Solver took to solve the problem
- The Solver Engine that was used and the Solver Options settings
- Where the Objective Cell was labeled in the Excel model for its name to appear as it does in Part 1 of the Answer Report
-

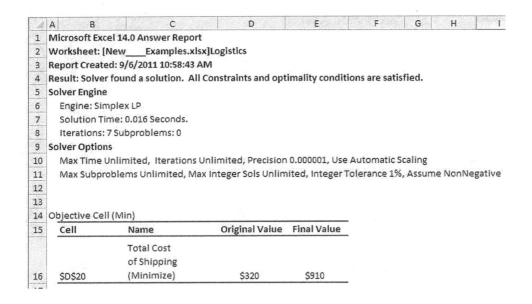

	A	B	C	D	E	F	G	H	I
1	Microsoft Excel 14.0 Answer Report								
2	Worksheet: [New____Examples.xlsx]Logistics								
3	Report Created: 9/6/2011 10:58:43 AM								
4	Result: Solver found a solution. All Constraints and optimality conditions are satisfied.								
5	Solver Engine								
6	Engine: Simplex LP								
7	Solution Time: 0.016 Seconds.								
8	Iterations: 7 Subproblems: 0								
9	Solver Options								
10	Max Time Unlimited, Iterations Unlimited, Precision 0.000001, Use Automatic Scaling								
11	Max Subproblems Unlimited, Max Integer Sols Unlimited, Integer Tolerance 1%, Assume NonNegative								
12									
13									
14	Objective Cell (Min)								
15	Cell	Name		Original Value	Final Value				
16	$D$20	Total Cost of Shipping (Minimize)		$320	$910				

Part 2

- Note that the Variable Cells contain the Decision Variables
- Note where the labels for each Decision Variable are placed in the Excel model so that the Decision Variable's name will appear here in Part 2 of the Answer Report as it does
- Note the type of variable - Either Continuous or Integer (Integer, Binary, or Alldifferent)
- Note the Before and After values of each Decision Variable

	A	B	C	D	E	F
18						
19	Variable Cells					
20		Cell	Name	Original Value	Final Value	Integer
21		$C$13	Factory 1 Number of Units Shipped To Store 1	10	20	Integer
22		$C$14	Factory 2 Number of Units Shipped To Store 1	10	0	Integer
23		$C$15	Factory 3 Number of Units Shipped To Store 1	10	90	Integer
24		$E$13	Factory 1 Number of Units Shipped To Store 2	10	40	Integer
25		$E$14	Factory 2 Number of Units Shipped To Store 2	10	0	Integer
26		$E$15	Factory 3 Number of Units Shipped To Store 2	10	0	Integer

	A	B	C	D	E	F
24		$E$13	Factory 1 Number of Units Shipped To Store 2	10	40	Integer
25		$E$14	Factory 2 Number of Units Shipped To Store 2	10	0	Integer
26		$E$15	Factory 3 Number of Units Shipped To Store 2	10	0	Integer
27		$G$13	Factory 1 Number of Units Shipped To Store 3	10	0	Integer
28		$G$14	Factory 2 Number of Units Shipped To Store 3	10	200	Integer
29		$G$15	Factory 3 Number of Units Shipped To Store 3	10	40	Integer
30						

Part 3

- Note how each Constraint is labeled in the Excel model in order for the Constraint's name to appear here in Part 3 of the Answer Report as it does
- Note which Constraints are binding (had their limits hit) and which aren't.
- Note how much slack is still available in any Constraint that has not had its limit hit.
- Note any Integer Constraints (Integer, Binary, Alldifferent)

	A	B	C	D	E	F	G
31							
32	Constraints						
33		Cell	Name	Cell Value	Formula	Status	Slack
34		$C$17	Total Number of Units Shipped To Store 1	110	$C$17=$B$28	Binding	0
35		$E$17	Total Number of Units Shipped To Store 2	40	$E$17=$B$29	Binding	0
36		$G$17	Total Number of Units Shipped To Store 3	240	$G$17=$B$30	Binding	0
37		$J$13	Factory 1 Total Units Shipped	60	$J$13<=$B$24	Not Binding	40
38		$J$14	Factory 2 Total Units Shipped	200	$J$14<=$B$25	Binding	0
39		$J$15	Factory 3 Total Units Shipped	130	$J$15<=$B$26	Binding	0

	A	B	C	D	E	F	G
40		$C$13=Integer					
41		$C$14=Integer					
42		$C$15=Integer					
43		$E$13=Integer					
44		$E$14=Integer					
45		$E$15=Integer					
46		$G$13=Integer					
47		$G$14=Integer					
48		$G$15=Integer					

Outbound Marketing Budget Optimization

Reaching a Required Number of Prospects As Cheaply As Possible With Outbound Marketing

This is a common corporate use of the Solver. The Solver is quite often used to select among outbound advertising media of varying Reach, Frequency, Ad Effectiveness, and Ad Cost to reach a maximum number of prospects while being constrained by the available advertising budget.

The Problem

A company must divide a limited outbound broadcast media advertising budget among 3 broadcast media vehicles in order to generate at least 1,000,000 Effective Advertising Impressions at the lowest total cost. The broadcast media vehicles are a local TV station and 2 cable TV stations.

Each of the 3 media vehicles is judged to have differing degrees of advertising effectiveness per each individual ad impression. This is due to differences in viewership demographics and relevancy of the programming to the company's advertising message. The number of ad impressions for each media vehicle is weighted according to vehicles effectiveness to produce a unit of measure called an Effective Advertising Impression.

Given the overall advertising budget and the maximum advertising spending per media vehicle, how should the overall advertising budget be divided up among the 3 broadcast media vehicles to produce at least 1,000,000 Effective Advertising Impression as cheaply as possible?

Specific details about each broadcast media vehicle are as follows:

	A	B	C	D	E
1					
2			Number of Advertising Broadcasts Needed To Obtain 1 Effective Advertising Impression	Reach - # of Viewers Likely Reached by Each Ad Broadcast	Cost Per Single Advertising Broadcast
3		TV Station	7	50,000	$195
4		Cable Station 1	4	40,000	$200
5		Cable Station 2	5	30,000	$175

Problem Solving Steps

Step 1 – Determine the Objective

In this case, the objective is to minimize the total amount spent on all 3 broadcast media vehicles in order to achieve at least 1,000,000 Effective Advertising Impressions. The total amount spent on advertising is the Objective that we are trying to reduce. The cell that calculates this total advertising expenditure is the Objective Cell.

Step 2 – Determine the Decision Variables

We are trying to determine how many ad broadcasts to perform with each of the 3 media vehicles in order to achieve at least 1,000,000 Effective Advertising Impressions at the lowest cost while staying within budget constraints. The numbers of ad broadcasts to perform with each broadcast media vehicle are the Decision Variables.

Step 3 – Build the Excel Equations That Combine the Objective With All Decision Variables

	A	B	C	D	E	F	G	H
1							Constraints	
2			Number of Advertising Broadcasts Needed To Obtain 1 Effective Advertising Impression	Reach - # of Viewers Likely Reached by Each Ad Broadcast	Cost Per Single Advertising Broadcast	Number of Ad Broadcasts	Ad Spend	Total Effective Advertising Impressions Per Advertising Vehicle
3		TV Station	7	50,000	$195	45	$8,775	321,429
4		Cable Station 1	4	40,000	$200	50	$10,000	500,000
5		Cable Station 2	5	30,000	$175	30	$5,250	180,000
6							Total Advertising Cost (Minimize)	Total Effective Advertising Impressions
7							$24,025	1,001,429
8							Objective	Constraint

Following is an expanded view of the left and right halves of the preceding Excel model for clarity. Here is the left half of the model:

	B	C	D	E
1				
2		Number of Advertising Broadcasts Needed To Obtain 1 Effective Advertising Impression	Reach - # of Viewers Likely Reached by Each Ad Broadcast	Cost Per Single Advertising Broadcast
3	TV Station	7	50,000	$195
4	Cable Station 1	4	40,000	$200
5	Cable Station 2	5	30,000	$175

Here is the right half of the model showing the interaction between the dark gray Decision Variables (F3 to F5), the light gray Objective Cell (G7), and the medium gray Constraints (G3 to G5, H7).

	F	G	H
1		Constraints	
2	Number of Ad Broadcasts	Ad Spend	Total Effective Advertising Impressions Per Advertising Vehicle
3	45	$8,775	321,429
4	50	$10,000	500,000
5	30	$5,250	180,000
6		Total Advertising Cost (Minimize)	Total Effective Advertising Impressions
7		$24,025	1,001,429
8		Objective	Constraint

The light gray Objective cell displays the total cost of advertising and will be minimized. The dark gray Decision Variable cells display the number of advertising broadcasts that will be made on each type of outbound media vehicle. The medium gray Constraint cells show the total ad spend for each advertising vehicle and the total number of Effective Advertising Impressions. These Constraint figures in the model are limited by the medium gray user Constraint inputs as follows in Step 4.

Step 4 – List all Constraints

	A	B	C	D	E	F	G
10							
11		**Constraints**					
12		$9,000	=	Total TV Advertising Budget ≥ TV Ad Spend			
13							
14		$10,000	=	Total Cable 1 Advertising Budget ≥ Cable 1 Ad Spend			
15							
16		$9,000	=	Total Cable 2 Advertising Budget ≥ Cable 2 Ad Spend			
17							
18		1,000,000	=	Minimum Effective Advertising Impressions			
19							
20							
21							
22		**Integer**		All 3 Decision Variables (green cells)			
23				(Number of Ad Broadcasts By Each Media Vehicle)			
24							
25		**Nonnegative**		All Unconstrained Variables			

The medium gray Constraint cells shown above are the cells that the user will input the maximum budgets for TV, Cable 1, and Cable 2. The final Constraint cell is the cell that the user will input the required minimum number Effective Advertising Impressions for the entire advertising campaign over all 3 media vehicles.

Step 5 – Test the Excel spreadsheet

Test the Excel spreadsheet completely before adding information to the Solver dialogue box. Make sure that any changes to Decision Variables or Constraints produce the correct results in the Objective cell.

Step 6 – Insert All Data into the Solver Dialogue Box

Input the Objective cell, Decision Variable cell, and all Constraints into the Solver dialogue box as follows:

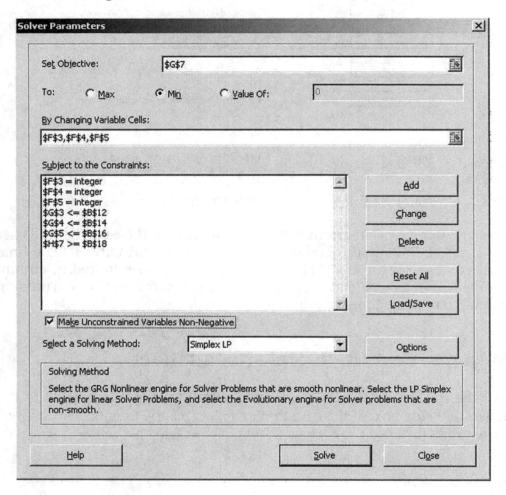

The Integer Constraints ensure that the ad broadcasts are performed in whole numbers. The inequality Constraints ensure that the ad spend per vehicle will not exceed that vehicle's budget and that at least the required number of Effective Advertising Impressions will be attained.

All equations on the Excel spreadsheet are linear (1st order) so we can use the Simplex LP (Linear Programming) Solver engine for this optimization problem.

Step 3 shows the completed problem with Decision Variables that have been optimized by the Solver to maximize the Objective while staying within the problem's Constraints.

Answer Report

Part 1

Note:
- The Solver Result
- How long Solver took to solve the problem
- The Solver Engine that was used and the Solver Options settings
- Where the Objective Cell was labeled in the Excel model for its name to appear as it does in Part 1 of the Answer Report

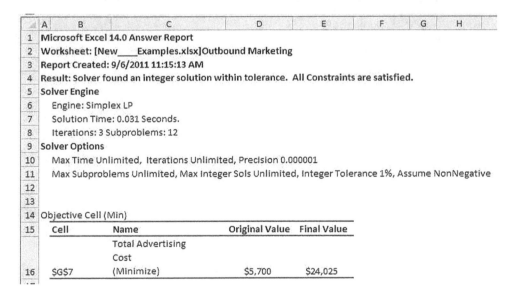

	A	B	C	D	E	F	G	H
1	Microsoft Excel 14.0 Answer Report							
2	Worksheet: [New____Examples.xlsx]Outbound Marketing							
3	Report Created: 9/6/2011 11:15:13 AM							
4	Result: Solver found an integer solution within tolerance. All Constraints are satisfied.							
5	Solver Engine							
6	Engine: Simplex LP							
7	Solution Time: 0.031 Seconds.							
8	Iterations: 3 Subproblems: 12							
9	Solver Options							
10	Max Time Unlimited, Iterations Unlimited, Precision 0.000001							
11	Max Subproblems Unlimited, Max Integer Sols Unlimited, Integer Tolerance 1%, Assume NonNegative							
12								
13								
14	Objective Cell (Min)							
15	Cell	Name		Original Value	Final Value			
16	$G$7	Total Advertising Cost (Minimize)		$5,700	$24,025			

Part 2

- Note that the Variable Cells contain the Decision Variables
- Note where the labels for each Decision Variable are placed in the Excel model so that the Decision Variable's name will appear here in Part 2 of the Answer Report as it does
- Note the type of variable - Either Continuous or Integer (**Integer**, Binary, or Alldifferent)
- Note the Before and After values of each Decision Variable

	A	B	C	D	E	F
19	Variable Cells					
20		Cell	Name	Original Value	Final Value	Integer
21		$F$3	TV Station Number of Ad Broadcasts	10	45	Integer
22		$F$4	Cable Station 1 Number of Ad Broadcasts	10	50	Integer
23		$F$5	Cable Station 2 Number of Ad Broadcasts	10	30	Integer

Part 3

- Note how each Constraint is labeled in the Excel model in order for the Constraint's name to appear here in Part 3 of the Answer Report as it does
- Note which Constraints are binding (had their limits hit) and which aren't.
- Note how much slack is still available in any Constraint that has not had its limit hit.
- Note any Integer Constraints (Integer, Binary, Alldifferent)

	A	B	C	D	E	F	G
25							
26	Constraints						
27		Cell	Name	Cell Value	Formula	Status	Slack
28		$G$3	TV Station Ad Spend	$8,775	$G$3<=$B$12	Not Binding	225
29		$G$4	Cable Station 1 Ad Spend	$10,000	$G$4<=$B$14	Binding	0
30		$G$5	Cable Station 2 Ad Spend	$5,250	$G$5<=$B$16	Not Binding	3750
31		$H$7	Total Effective Advertising Impressions	1,001,429	$H$7>=$B$18	Not Binding	1,429
32		$F$3=Integer					
33		$F$4=Integer					
34		$F$5=Integer					

Inbound Marketing Budget Optimization

Generating a Required Number of Qualified Leads Using Inbound Marketing As Cheaply As Possible

The Solver has always been a widely used tool to allocate an advertising budget among outbound broadcast media vehicles of varying Reach, Frequency, and cost. The Solver can also be used just as effectively to allocate a marketing budget among inbound Internet marketing vehicles.

In this problem, a pay-per-click marketing budget will be divided up among 3 pay-per-click advertising vehicles in order to generate the highest number of qualified leads. Each of the 3 different pay-per-click vehicles has a different cost and effectiveness per click.

The Problem

An overall Inbound Marketing budget must be divided among 3 pay-per-click vehicles in order to achieve the highest number of qualified leads. In addition to an overall budget limit, each pay-per-click vehicle has an advertising spending limit as well.

The 3 pay-per-click vehicles are AdWords, Facebook, and LinkedIn. Each one of these has a different cost-per-click and also has a different effectiveness. The objective is to divide the overall Inbound Marketing advertising budget among these 3 pay-per-click vehicles to achieve the highest number of qualified leads.

Following are the specific details about the cost and effectiveness of each of the 3 pay-per-click advertising vehicles:

	A	B	C	D	E
1					
2			Average Cost Per Click	Average Number of Clicks Needed To Obtain 1 Active Inquiry	Average Number of Inquiries Needed To Obtain 1 Qualified Lead
3		AdWords	$0.15	5	6
4		Facebook	$0.18	4	8
5		LInkedIn	$0.25	3	7
6					

Problem Solving Steps

Step 1 – Determine the Objective

In this case, the objective is to maximize the total number of qualified leads. The total number of leads is therefore the Objective. The cell that calculates that total number of Qualified Leads obtained is the Objective Cell.

Step 2 – Determine the Decision Variables

We are trying to determine how much money to spend on each pay-per-click vehicle in order to maximize the total number of qualified leads while not exceeding the given budget   constraints. The Decision Variables are the amounts of money to spend on each pay-per-click vehicle.

Step 3 – Build the Excel Equations That Combine the Objective With All Decision Variables

	A	B	C	D	E	F	G	H	I	J
7										
8			Ad Spend	Average Cost Per Click	Expected Number of Clicks For the Given Ad Spend	Average Number of Clicks Needed To Obtain 1 Active Inquiry	Expected Number of Active Inquiries	Average Number of Inquiries Needed To Obtain 1 Qualified Lead	Expected Number of Qualified Leads	
9		AdWords	$1,250	$0.15	188	5	38	6	6	
10		Facebook	$750	$0.18	135	4	34	8	4	
11		LinkedIn	$3,000	$0.25	750	3	250	7	36	
12			Decision Variables (Are Also Constrained)							
13			Total Ad Spend						Total Expected Number of Qualified Leads (Maximize)	
14			$5,000						46	
			Constraint						Objective	

The light gray Objective cell (i14) displays the total number of number of expected qualified leads. The dark gray Decision Variable cells (C9 to C11) display the amounts of money (ad spend) spent on each of the pay-per-click vehicles to achieve the objective.

Step 4 – List all Constraints

	B	C	D	E	F	G	H
17							
18		Constraints					
19		$5,000	=	Total Advertising Budget ≥ Total Ad Spend			
20							
21		$3,000	=	Total AdWords Budget ≥ AdWords Ad Spend			
22							
23		$750	=	Total Facebook Budget ≥ Facebook Ad Spend			
24							
25		$3,000	=	Total LinkedIn Budget ≥ LinkedIn Ad Spend			
26							
27							
28							
29		Integer		All 3 Decision Variables (green cells)			
30				(Ad Spend For Each Pay-Per-Click Vehicle)			
31							
32		Nonnegative		All Unconstrained Variables			

The preceding medium gray Constraint cells link to the model to limit total ad spend and ad spend for each pay-per-click vehicle.

Step 5 – Test the Excel spreadsheet

Test the Excel spreadsheet completely before adding information to the Solver dialogue box. Make sure that any changes to dark gray Decision Variables produce the correct results in the light gray Objective cell.

Step 6 – Insert All Data into the Solver Dialogue Box

Input the Objective cell, Decision Variable cell, and all Constraints into the Solver dialogue box as follows:

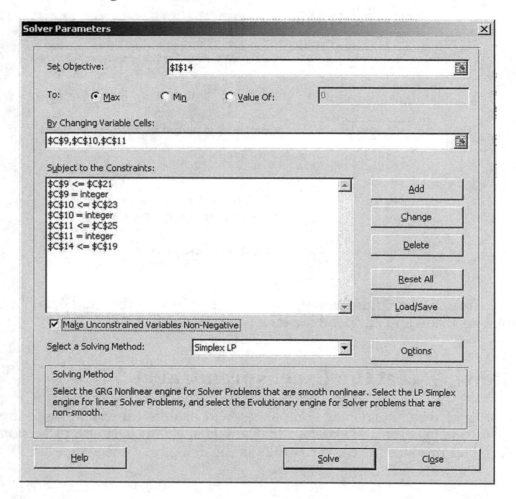

Integer Constraints ensure that ad spend is kept in whole dollar amounts. Inequality Constraints ensure that ad budgets are not exceeded.

All equations on the Excel spreadsheet are linear (1st order) so we can use the Simplex LP (Linear Programming) Solver engine for this optimization problem.

Step 3 shows the completed problem with Decision Variables that have been optimized by the Solver to maximize the Objective while staying within the problem's Constraints.

Answer Report

Part 1

Note:
- The Solver Result
- How long Solver took to solve the problem
- The Solver Engine that was used and the Solver Options settings
- Where the Objective Cell was labeled in the Excel model for its name to appear as it does in Part 1 of the Answer Report

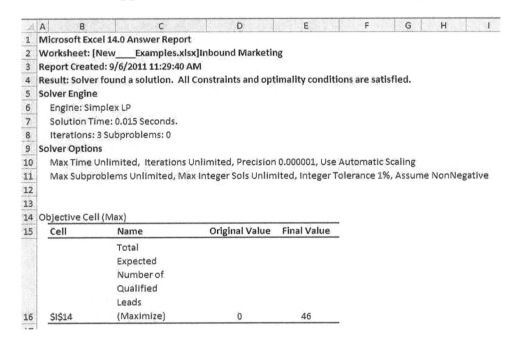

	A	B	C	D	E	F	G	H	I
1	Microsoft Excel 14.0 Answer Report								
2	Worksheet: [New___Examples.xlsx]Inbound Marketing								
3	Report Created: 9/6/2011 11:29:40 AM								
4	Result: Solver found a solution. All Constraints and optimality conditions are satisfied.								
5	Solver Engine								
6	Engine: Simplex LP								
7	Solution Time: 0.015 Seconds.								
8	Iterations: 3 Subproblems: 0								
9	Solver Options								
10	Max Time Unlimited, Iterations Unlimited, Precision 0.000001, Use Automatic Scaling								
11	Max Subproblems Unlimited, Max Integer Sols Unlimited, Integer Tolerance 1%, Assume NonNegative								
12									
13									
14	Objective Cell (Max)								
15	Cell	Name		Original Value	Final Value				
16	$I$14	Total Expected Number of Qualified Leads (Maximize)		0	46				

Part 2

- Note that the Variable Cells contain the Decision Variables
- Note where the labels for each Decision Variable are placed in the Excel model so that the Decision Variable's name will appear here in Part 2 of the Answer Report as it does
- Note the type of variable - Either Continuous or Integer (**Integer**, Binary, or Alldifferent)
- Note the Before and After values of each Decision Variable

	A	B	C	D	E	F
19	Variable Cells					
20	Cell	Name	Original Value	Final Value	Integer
21	$C$9	AdWords Ad Spend	$10	$1,250	Integer
22	$C$10	Facebook Ad Spend	$10	$750	Integer
23	$C$11	LinkedIn Ad Spend	$10	$3,000	Integer
24						

Part 3

- Note how each Constraint is labeled in the Excel model in order for the Constraint's name to appear here in Part 3 of the Answer Report as it does
- Note which Constraints are binding (had their limits hit) and which aren't.
- Note how much slack is still available in any Constraint that has not had its limit hit.
- Note any Integer Constraints (Integer, Binary, Alldifferent)

	A	B	C	D	E	F	G
25							
26	Constraints						
27		Cell	Name	Cell Value	Formula	Status	Slack
28		$C$14	Total Ad Spend	$5,000	$C$14<=$C$19	Binding	0
29		$C$11	LinkedIn Ad Spend	$3,000	$C$11<=$C$25	Binding	0
30		$C$10	Facebook Ad Spend	$750	$C$10<=$C$23	Binding	0
31		$C$9	AdWords Ad Spend	$1,250	$C$9<=$C$21	Not Binding	1750
32		$C$10=Integer					
33		$C$11=Integer					
34		$C$9=Integer					
35							

Bond Portfolio Optimization Example

Optimizing the Allocation of Bonds in a Portfolio To Maximize Return

One basic use of the Solver is to correctly divide a bond portfolio among bonds of different yield, maturity, and risk or in order to maximize yield or minimize risk.

The Problem

Correctly divide a bond portfolio among 4 bonds of varying yields and maturities in order to achieve an overall bond portfolio with an average maturity of 5.5 years while maximizing overall yield.

Specific information about each bond is as follows:

	A	B	C	D
1				
2			Bond Duration (Years)	Bond Yield
3		Bond 1	4	7%
4		Bond 2	5	8%
5		Bond 3	6	9%
6		Bond 4	3	6%

Problem Solving Steps

Step 1 – Determine the Objective

In this case, the Objective is to create a portfolio that maximizes the overall portfolio yield while having a specific average maturity. The Objective is the overall yield of the entire portfolio. The cell that calculates this overall yield is the Objective Cell.

Step 2 – Determine the Decision Variables

We are trying to determine what percentage of the overall portfolio to allocate to each bond in order to maximize the total yield while maintaining an average maturity of 5.5 years. The Decision Variables are the percentages of the overall portfolio that are allocated to bond type.

Step 3 – Build the Excel Equations That Combine the Objective With All Decision Variables

	A	B	C	D	E	F	G
1					Decision Variables		
2			Bond Duration (Years)	Bond Yield	Portfolio Percentage	Duration X Portfolio Percentage	Yield X Portfolio Percentage
3		Bond 1	4	7%	0%	0	0.00%
4		Bond 2	5	8%	0%	0	0.00%
5		Bond 3	6	9%	83%	5	7.50%
6		Bond 4	3	6%	17%	0.5	1.00%
7					Total Portfolio Held (Should Add Up To 100%)	Total Target Bond Portfolio Duration (Years)	Total Bond Portfolio Yield (Maximize)
8					100%	5.5	8.50%
						Constraint	Objective

The light gray Objective cell G8 displays the overall portfolio yield and will be maximized. The dark gray Decision Variable cells (E3 to E6) display the percentages of the overall portfolio to achieve the objective while creating a portfolio with an average maturity of 5.5 years. The medium gray Constraint cell in the model (F8) establishes the average bond maturity and is controlled by the medium gray user input in cell B12 in the following diagram:

Step 4 – List all Constraints

	A	B	C	D	E	F	G
10							
11		Constraints					
12		5.5	=	Total Target Bond Portfolio Duration (Years)			
13							
14							
15							
16		Nonnegative		All Unconstrained Variables			

Step 5 – Test the Excel spreadsheet

Test the Excel spreadsheet completely before adding information to the Solver dialogue box. Make sure that any changes to dark gray Decision Variables produce the correct results in the light gray Objective cell.

Step 6 – Insert All Data into the Solver Dialogue Box

Input the Objective cell, Decision Variable cell, and all Constraints into the Solver dialogue box as follows:

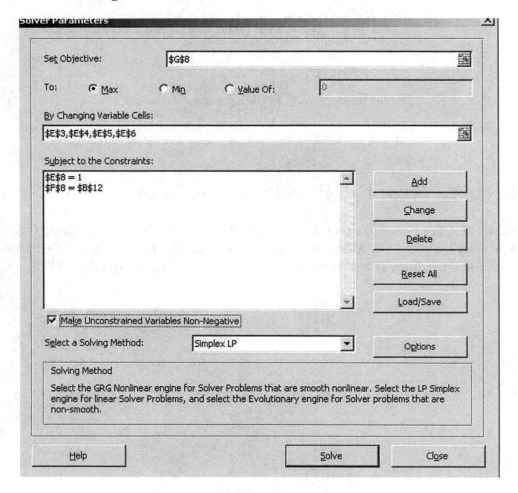

All equations on the Excel spreadsheet are linear (1st order) so we can use the Simplex LP (Linear Programming) method for this optimization problem.

Step 3 shows the completed problem with Decision Variables that have been optimized by the Solver to maximize the Objective while staying within the problem's Constraints.

Answer Report

Part 1

Note:

- The Solver Result
- How long Solver took to solve the problem
- The Solver Engine that was used and the Solver Options settings
- Where the Objective Cell was labeled in the Excel model for its name to appear as it does in Part 1 of the Answer Report

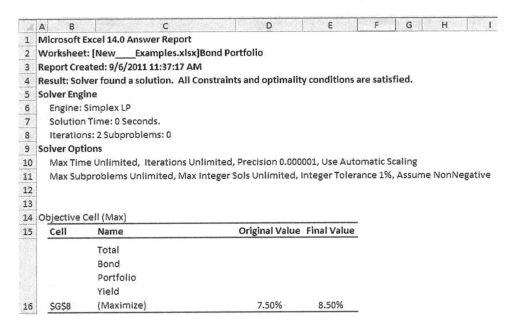

	A	B	C	D	E	F	G	H	I
1	Microsoft Excel 14.0 Answer Report								
2	Worksheet: [New____Examples.xlsx]Bond Portfolio								
3	Report Created: 9/6/2011 11:37:17 AM								
4	Result: Solver found a solution. All Constraints and optimality conditions are satisfied.								
5	Solver Engine								
6	Engine: Simplex LP								
7	Solution Time: 0 Seconds.								
8	Iterations: 2 Subproblems: 0								
9	Solver Options								
10	Max Time Unlimited, Iterations Unlimited, Precision 0.000001, Use Automatic Scaling								
11	Max Subproblems Unlimited, Max Integer Sols Unlimited, Integer Tolerance 1%, Assume NonNegative								
12									
13									
14	Objective Cell (Max)								
15	Cell	Name		Original Value	Final Value				
16	$G$8	Total Bond Portfolio Yield (Maximize)		7.50%	8.50%				

Part 2

- Note that the Variable Cells contain the Decision Variables
- Note where the labels for each Decision Variable are placed in the Excel model so that the Decision Variable's name will appear here in Part 2 of the Answer Report as it does
- Note the type of variable - Either **Continuous** or Integer (Integer, Binary, or Alldifferent)
- Note the Before and After values of each Decision Variable
-

	A	B	C	D	E	F
19	Variable Cells					
20		Cell	Name	Original Value	Final Value	Integer
21		$E$3	Bond 1 Portfolio Percentage	25%	0%	Contin
22		$E$4	Bond 2 Portfolio Percentage	25%	0%	Contin
23		$E$5	Bond 3 Portfolio Percentage	25%	83%	Contin
24		$E$6	Bond 4 Portfolio Percentage	25%	17%	Contin

Part 3

- Note how each Constraint is labeled in the Excel model in order for the Constraint's name to appear here in Part 3 of the Answer Report as it does
- Note which Constraints are binding (had their limits hit) and which aren't.
- Note how much slack is still available in any Constraint that has not had its limit hit.
- Note any Integer Constraints (Integer, Binary, Alldifferent)

	A	B	C	D	E	F	G
25							
26							
27	Constraints						
28		Cell	Name	Cell Value	Formula	Status	Slack
29		$E$8	Total Portfolio Held (Should Add Up To 100%)	100%	$E$8=1	Binding	0
30		$F$8	Total Target Bond Portfolio Duration (Years)	5.5	$F$8=$B$12	Binding	0

Limits Report

The Limits Report is made available when the Solver finds a Globally or Locally Optimal solution and no Integer Constraints (Integer, Binary, Alldifferent) were used. Part 2 of the Answer Report Shows that the variables were Continuous and not Integers. The Simplex LP method solves linear problems to globally optimal solutions.

The 2nd section of the Limits Report just shown indicates that none of the Decision Variables have any slack because the upper and lower limits of each Decision Variable are the same.

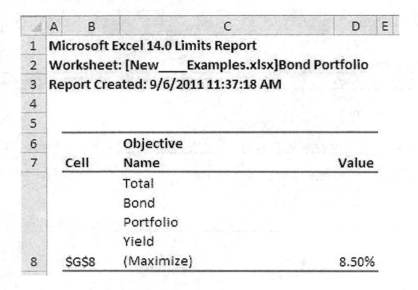

	A	B	C	D	E
1	Microsoft Excel 14.0 Limits Report				
2	Worksheet: [New____Examples.xlsx]Bond Portfolio				
3	Report Created: 9/6/2011 11:37:18 AM				
4					
5					
6		Objective			
7	Cell	Name		Value	
8	$G$8	Total Bond Portfolio Yield (Maximize)		8.50%	

	A	B	C	D	E	F	G	H	I	J
10										
11			Variable			Lower	Objective		Upper	Objective
12		Cell	Name	Value		Limit	Result		Limit	Result
13		$E$3	Bond 1 Portfolio Percentage	0%		0%	8.50%		0%	8.50%
14		$E$4	Bond 2 Portfolio Percentage	0%		0%	8.50%		0%	8.50%
15		$E$5	Bond 3 Portfolio Percentage	83%		83%	8.50%		83%	8.50%
16		$E$6	Bond 4 Portfolio Percentage	17%		17%	8.50%		17%	8.50%

Sensitivity Report

The Sensitivity Report is also made available when the Solver finds a Globally or Locally Optimal solution and no Integer Constraints (Integer, Binary, Alldifferent) were used. Part 2 of the Answer Report Shows that the variables were Continuous and not Integers. The Simplex LP method solves linear problems to globally optimal solutions.

Microsoft Excel 14.0 Sensitivity Report
Worksheet: [New____Examples.xlsx]Bond Portfolio
Report Created: 9/6/2011 11:37:18 AM

Variable Cells

Cell	Name	Final Value	Reduced Cost	Objective Coefficient	Allowable Increase	Allowable Decrease
$E$3	Bond 1 Portfolio Percentage	0	-1.04083E-17	0.07	1.04083E-17	1E+30
$E$4	Bond 2 Portfolio Percentage	0	0	0.08	0	1E+30
$E$5	Bond 3 Portfolio Percentage	0.833333333	0	0.09	1E+30	0
$E$6	Bond 4 Portfolio Percentage	0.166666667	0	0.06	1E+30	0

Constraints

Cell	Name	Final Value	Shadow Price	Constraint R.H. Side	Allowable Increase	Allowable Decrease
$E$8	Total Portfolio Held (Should Add Up To 100%)	1	0.03	1	0.833333333	0.083333333
$F$8	Total Target Bond Portfolio Duration (Years)	5.5	0.01	5.5	0.5	2.5

Optimal Investment Selection Example

Maximizing Investment Return Through Optimal Investment Selection Using the Binary Constraint

The Solver can be used to maximize return when selecting investments with a limited amount of investment capital. Projected cash flows for each investment are Solver inputs. Binary Decision Variables determining whether or not an investment will be made. The Solver calculates the Net Present Value of each possible combination of investments and determines the investment combination that maximizes Net Present Value (NPV) of invested cash flows.

The Problem

A venture capitalist with limited funds can make annual investments over the next 2 years. He has 6 investment opportunites to choose from. 3 of the investment opportunities will occur at the start of year 1. The other 3 investment opportunities will occur at the start of year 2. He doesn't have to invest anything if he chooses not to. If he does choose to invest in any opportunity, he must invest upfront 100% of start-up capital required by that investment. The venture capitalist has only enough capital to make 2 investments during any one year.

The projected annual cash flows for each investment are shown below. These projected cash flows include the upfront investment that the venture capitalist would have to make.

The goal is to select the investments that would maximize Net Present Value at year 0 of all cash flows of all selected investments.

A discount rate of 25% will be used because the investments are considered risky.

The projected annual cash flows for each investment, including all upfront investments, are shown as follows:

	A	B	C	D	E	F	G	H
1								
2			Projected Annual Cash Flows of All Possible Investments - Including First Year Upfront Investment					
3								
4			Year 1 Opportunity 1	Year 1 Opportunity 2	Year 1 Opportunity 3	Year 2 Opportunity 1	Year 2 Opportunity 2	Year 2 Opportunity 3
5		Year 1	($70,000)	($80,000)	($90,000)			
6		Year 2	($10,000)	($20,000)	($15,000)	($80,000)	($90,000)	($100,000)
7		Year 3	($5,000)	($15,000)	($10,000)	($10,000)	($10,000)	($25,000)
8		Year 4	$65,000	$45,000	$20,000	$2,000	$5,000	($5,000)
9		Year 5	$180,000	$150,000	$140,000	$25,000	$190,000	$10,000
10		Year 6	$280,000	$250,000	$250,000	$175,000	$250,000	$45,000

Problem Solving Steps

Step 1 – Determine the Objective

In this case, the objective is to maximize the Net Present Value at Year 0 of all cash flows of all selected investments. The cell in which the Net Present Value at Year 0 is calculated is the Objective Cell.

Step 2 – Determine the Decision Variables

We are trying to select the investments which will produce the highest Net Present Value of all cash flows at Year 0. The Decision Variables are binary variables (taking values of 1 or 0) which indicate whether an investment opportunity was chosen.

Step 3 – Build the Excel Equations That Combine the Objective With All Decision Variables

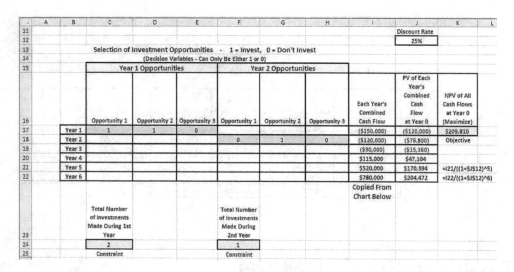

On the following pages are expanded views of the left and right sides of the preceding Excel model for better clarity.

Shown as follows is the left side of the Excel model. The dark gray Decision Variables (C17 to E17, F18 to H18) are binary variables occurring in Years 1 and 2. The medium gray Constraints cell (C24 and F24) limit the maximum number of investments that can be made during Year 1 and Year 2.

	A	B	C	D	E	F	G	H
13			Selection of Investment Opportunities - 1 = Invest, 0 = Don't Invest					
14			(Decision Variables - Can Only Be Either 1 or 0)					
15			Year 1 Opportunities			Year 2 Opportunities		
16			Opportunity 1	Opportunity 2	Opportunity 3	Opportunity 1	Opportunity 2	Opportunity 3
17		Year 1	1	1	0			
18		Year 2				0	1	0
19		Year 3						
20		Year 4						
21		Year 5						
22		Year 6						
23			Total Number of Investments Made During 1st Year			Total Number of Investments Made During 2nd Year		
24			2			1		
25			Constraint			Constraint		

The right side of the model shown as follows contains 1) the combined annual cash flows for all selected investments (Column I), 2) the Present Value at Year 0 of each combined annual cash flow (Column J), 3) and the light gray Objective cell (K17) containing the Net Present Value at Year 0 of all combined annual cash flows (the sum of the Year 0 Present Values). Each year's combined cash flows (I17 to I22) were copied from cells I31 to I36. The Excel formula for calculating the Present Values at Year 0 in column J is also shown.

	I	J	K	L
11		Discount Rate		
12		25%		
13				
14				
15				
16	Each Year's Combined Cash Flow	PV of Each Year's Combined Cash Flow at Year 0	NPV of All Cash Flows at Year 0 (Maximize)	
17	($150,000)	($120,000)	$209,810	
18	($120,000)	($76,800)	Objective	
19	($30,000)	($15,360)		
20	$115,000	$47,104		
21	$520,000	$170,394	=I21/((1+$J$12)^5)	
22	$780,000	$204,472	=I22/((1+$J$12)^6)	
	Copied From Chart Below			

	A	B	C	D	E	F	G	H	I
27									
28		Cash Flows As a Result of Investment Selections							
29		Cell C31 Contains this If-Then-Else Statement: =IF($C$17=1,C5," ") All Cells From C31 To I36 Contain Similar Formulas							
30			Year 1 Opportunity 1	Year 1 Opportunity 2	Year 1 Opportunity 3	Year 2 Opportunity 1	Year 2 Opportunity 2	Year 2 Opportunity 3	Combined Cash Flow
31		Year 1	($70,000)	($80,000)					($150,000)
32		Year 2	($10,000)	($20,000)			($90,000)		($120,000)
33		Year 3	($5,000)	($15,000)			($10,000)		($30,000)
34		Year 4	$65,000	$45,000			$5,000		$115,000
35		Year 5	$180,000	$150,000			$190,000		$520,000
36		Year 6	$280,000	$250,000			$250,000		$780,000

Calculation of Net Present Value (NPV) of All Cash Flows At Year 0

The Net Present value (NPV) of all cash flows at year 0 equals the sum of the Present Value (PV) of each total annual cash flow at Year 0.

The Present Value at Year 0 of a cash flow that occurs in Year t is:

$$PV_{t=0} = C_t(1 + i)^{-t}$$

C_t = Cash flow C that occurs in year t

I = Discount rate – We are discounting all cash flows back using a discount rate of 25% because the investment is considered risky, as most venture capital investments are. The Discount Rate is user-controlled.

For example, the Present Value at Year 0 of the Year 4 Cash flow, $115,000, would be calculated as follows:

$$PV_{t=0} = C_t(1 + i)^{-t}$$

$$PV_{t=0} = (\$115,000)(1 + 0.25)^{-4} = \$47,104$$

The light gray Objective cell displays the Net Present Value of all annual cash flows of all selected investments. This Objective cell will be maximized. The dark gray Decision Variable cells are binary and indicate whether or not a particular Year 1 or Year 2 investment opportunity has been chosen.

How To Display Only the Cash flows of the Selected Investments

The Objective of this problem is to select the combination of investments that produce the highest Net Present Value at Year 0. In order to calculate the NPV at Year 0 of all projected cash flows in the selected investments, we must find a method to display only the projected cash flows from the selected investments so that we can perform analysis on only these cash flows.

Here is one simple way to do that. First, we must list the projected cash flows of all 6 possible investment opportunities, as shown as follows:

	A	B	C	D	E	F	G	H
1								
2		Projected Annual Cash Flows of All Possible Investments - Including First Year Upfront Investment						
3								
4			Year 1 Opportunity 1	Year 1 Opportunity 2	Year 1 Opportunity 3	Year 2 Opportunity 1	Year 2 Opportunity 2	Year 2 Opportunity 3
5		Year 1	($70,000)	($80,000)	($90,000)			
6		Year 2	($10,000)	($20,000)	($15,000)	($80,000)	($90,000)	($100,000)
7		Year 3	($5,000)	($15,000)	($10,000)	($10,000)	($10,000)	($25,000)
8		Year 4	$65,000	$45,000	$20,000	$2,000	$5,000	($5,000)
9		Year 5	$180,000	$150,000	$140,000	$25,000	$190,000	$10,000
10		Year 6	$280,000	$250,000	$250,000	$175,000	$250,000	$45,000

		Year 1 Opportunity 1	Year 1 Opportunity 2	Year 1 Opportunity 3	Year 2 Opportunity 1	Year 2 Opportunity 2	Year 2 Opportunity 3	Combined Cash Flow
27									
28		Cash Flows As a Result of Investment Selections							
29		Cell C31 Contains this If-Then-Else Statement: =IF($C$17=1,C5," ")			All Cells From C31 To I36 Contain Similar Formulas				
31	Year 1	($70,000)	($80,000)					($150,000)
32	Year 2	($10,000)	($20,000)			($90,000)		($120,000)
33	Year 3	($5,000)	($15,000)			($10,000)		($30,000)
34	Year 4	$65,000	$45,000			$5,000		$115,000
35	Year 5	$180,000	$150,000			$190,000		$520,000
36	Year 6	$280,000	$250,000			$250,000		$780,000

Now we need to display the cells containing the binary Decision Variables which indicate whether or not an investment has been selected. This is shown as follows, along with an expanded view of those Decision Variables:

		Year 1 Opportunities			Year 2 Opportunities			Each Year's Combined Cash Flow	PV of Each Year's Combined Cash Flow at Year 0	NPV of All Cash Flows at Year 0 (Maximize)
11									Discount Rate	
12									25%	
13		Selection of Investment Opportunities - 1 = Invest, 0 = Don't Invest								
14		(Decision Variables - Can Only Be Either 1 or 0)								
15										
16		Opportunity 1	Opportunity 2	Opportunity 3	Opportunity 1	Opportunity 2	Opportunity 3			
17	Year 1	1	1	0				($150,000)	($120,000)	$209,810
18	Year 2				0	1	0	($120,000)	($76,800)	Objective
19	Year 3							($30,000)	($15,360)	
20	Year 4							$115,000	$47,104	
21	Year 5							$520,000	$170,394	=I21/((1+$J$12)^5)
22	Year 6							$780,000	$204,472	=I22/((1+$J$12)^6)
								Copied From Chart Below		
23		Total Number of Investments Made During 1st Year			Total Number of Investments Made During 2nd Year					
24		2			1					
25		Constraint			Constraint					

An expanded view of those binary Decision Variables is shown as follows:

	A	B	C	D	E	F	G	H
13			Selection of Investment Opportunities - 1 = Invest, 0 = Don't Invest					
14			(Decision Variables - Can Only Be Either 1 or 0)					
15			Year 1 Opportunities			Year 2 Opportunities		
16			Opportunity 1	Opportunity 2	Opportunity 3	Opportunity 1	Opportunity 2	Opportunity 3
17		Year 1	1	1	0			
18		Year 2				0	1	0
19		Year 3						
20		Year 4						
21		Year 5						
22		Year 6						
23			Total Number of Investments Made During 1st Year			Total Number of Investments Made During 2nd Year		
24			2			1		
25			Constraint			Constraint		

We can now display only the annuals projected cash flows that are connected with selected investments. This can be done very efficiently in Excel with an If-Then-Else statement.

The end result of using If-Then-Else statements is shown as follows. Each of the cells in the following spreadsheet portion contains an If-Then-Else statement. Each of these If-Then-Else statements copies the cash flow from the same location in the list of all projected cash flows above only if that respective opportunity has been selected.

In other words, the cash flow will be copied down only if the Decision Variable cell for that investment opportunity contains a 1, meaning that investment has been selected.

	A	B	C	D	E	F	G	H	I
27									
28		Cash Flows As a Result of Investment Selections							
29		Cell C31 Contains this If-Then-Else Statement: =IF($C$17=1,C5," ")				All Cells From C31 To I36 Contain Similar Formulas			
30			Year 1 Opportunity 1	Year 1 Opportunity 2	Year 1 Opportunity 3	Year 2 Opportunity 1	Year 2 Opportunity 2	Year 2 Opportunity 3	Combined Cash Flow
31		Year 1	($70,000)	($80,000)					($150,000)
32		Year 2	($10,000)	($20,000)			($90,000)		($120,000)
33		Year 3	($5,000)	($15,000)			($10,000)		($30,000)
34		Year 4	$65,000	$45,000			$5,000		$115,000
35		Year 5	$180,000	$150,000			$190,000		$520,000
36		Year 6	$280,000	$250,000			$250,000		$780,000

For example, in cell C31 of the Excel model in the preceding image is the following If-Then-Else code:

=if($C$17=1,C5," ")

This Excel statement copies the cash flow from C5 into C31 only Decision Variable cell C17 is set to 1, which indicates that this investment has been selected.

This formula is copied from Cell 31 into all cells down and over to Cell C36. Note that Cell $C$17 is made to be an absolute reference because of the dollar signs. All of the copied formulas from cell C31 to Cell C36 will depend on whether Cell C17 contains a 1 or a 0.

The formula is also copied over and down to Cell I36. In each column, the absolute reference is move over. For example, all Cells from D31 to D36 now have absolute references on the Cell $D$17. Take a look at the contents of those cells in the downloadable spreadsheet containing this example. This concept is probably easier to understand when scrolling through the actual Excel spreadsheet.

If this investment was not selected, its Decision Variable cell C17 would be set to 0 and nothing (" ") would be copied into cell C31. In this way, only cash flows of selected investment appear once again in the image on the following page:

		Year 1 Opportunity 1	Year 1 Opportunity 2	Year 1 Opportunity 3	Year 2 Opportunity 1	Year 2 Opportunity 2	Year 2 Opportunity 3	Combined Cash Flow
27								
28	Cash Flows As a Result of Investment Selections							
29	Cell C31 Contains this If-Then-Else Statement: =IF($C$17=1,C5," ") All Cells From C31 To I36 Contain Similar Formulas							
30								
31	Year 1	($70,000)	($80,000)					($150,000)
32	Year 2	($10,000)	($20,000)			($90,000)		($120,000)
33	Year 3	($5,000)	($15,000)			($10,000)		($30,000)
34	Year 4	$65,000	$45,000			$5,000		$115,000
35	Year 5	$180,000	$150,000			$190,000		$520,000
36	Year 6	$280,000	$250,000			$250,000		$780,000

All annual cash flows for the selected investments are summed up in the right column in Cells I31 to I36 as just shown.

These combined cash flows are copied back into the right side (Cell I31 to I36 are copied into I17 to I22) of the spreadsheet section containing the Decision Variable cells shown as follows:

		Opportunity 1	Opportunity 2	Opportunity 3	Opportunity 1	Opportunity 2	Opportunity 3	Each Year's Combined Cash Flow	PV of Each Year's Combined Cash Flow at Year 0	NPV of All Cash Flows at Year 0 (Maximize)	
11										Discount Rate	
12										25%	
13		Selection of Investment Opportunities - 1 = Invest, 0 = Don't Invest									
14		(Decision Variables - Can Only Be Either 1 or 0)									
15		Year 1 Opportunities			Year 2 Opportunities						
16		Opportunity 1	Opportunity 2	Opportunity 3	Opportunity 1	Opportunity 2	Opportunity 3	Each Year's Combined Cash Flow	PV of Each Year's Combined Cash Flow at Year 0	NPV of All Cash Flows at Year 0 (Maximize)	
17	Year 1	1	1	0				($150,000)	($120,000)	$209,810	
18	Year 2				0	1	0	($120,000)	($76,800)	Objective	
19	Year 3							($30,000)	($15,360)		
20	Year 4							$115,000	$47,104		
21	Year 5							$520,000	$170,394	=I21/((1+$J$12)^5)	
22	Year 6							$780,000	$204,472	=I22/((1+$J$12)^6)	
23		Total Number of Investments Made During 1st Year			Total Number of Investments Made During 2nd Year			Copied From Chart Below			
24		2			1						
25		Constraint			Constraint						

Here is an expanded view of the left side of the previous spreadsheet:

	A	B	C	D	E	F	G	H
13			Selection of Investment Opportunities - 1 = Invest, 0 = Don't Invest					
14			(Decision Variables - Can Only Be Either 1 or 0)					
15			Year 1 Opportunities			Year 2 Opportunities		
16			Opportunity 1	Opportunity 2	Opportunity 3	Opportunity 1	Opportunity 2	Opportunity 3
17		Year 1	1	1	0			
18		Year 2				0	1	0
19		Year 3						
20		Year 4						
21		Year 5						
22		Year 6						
23			Total Number of Investments Made During 1st Year			Total Number of Investments Made During 2nd Year		
24			2			1		
25			Constraint			Constraint		

Shown as follows is an expanded view of the right side of the Excel model. You can see the cash flows in I17 to I22 that have been copied from I31 to I36:

	I	J	K	L
11		Discount Rate		
12		25%		
13				
14				
15				
16	Each Year's Combined Cash Flow	PV of Each Year's Combined Cash Flow at Year 0	NPV of All Cash Flows at Year 0 (Maximize)	
17	($150,000)	($120,000)	$209,810	
18	($120,000)	($76,800)	Objective	
19	($30,000)	($15,360)		
20	$115,000	$47,104		
21	$520,000	$170,394	=I21/((1+$J$12)^5)	
22	$780,000	$204,472	=I22/((1+$J$12)^6)	
	Copied From Chart Below			

The user can change the Discount Rate here and watch the spreadsheet calculations immediately change to reflect the new Discount Rate. The greater the Discount Rate, the greater that the investment risk is believed to be and the lower will be the NPV of the cash flows at Year 0 of the selected investments.

The PV and NPV calculations are performed on these cash flow figures to attain the Objective, which is the NPV at Year 0 of all projected cash flows of all selected investments.

Step 4 – List all Constraints

	B	C	D	E	F	G
39						
40		Constraints				
41						
42		Binary		All 6 Decision Variables (green cells)		
43						
44						
45		Nonnegative		All Unconstrained Variables		
46						
47						
48		Only 2 Investments Can be Made During Any Year				

Step 5 – Test the Excel spreadsheet

Test the Excel spreadsheet completely before adding information to the Solver dialogue box. Make sure that any changes to Decision Variables produce the correct results in the Objective cell.

Step 6 – Insert All Data into the Solver Dialogue Box

Input the Objective cell, Decision Variable cell, and all Constraints into the Solver dialogue box. Note that the Binary Constraint was applied to the 6 Yes-or-No Decision Variables. The inequality Constraints limit the maximum number of investments to 2 in each of Year 1 and Year 2.

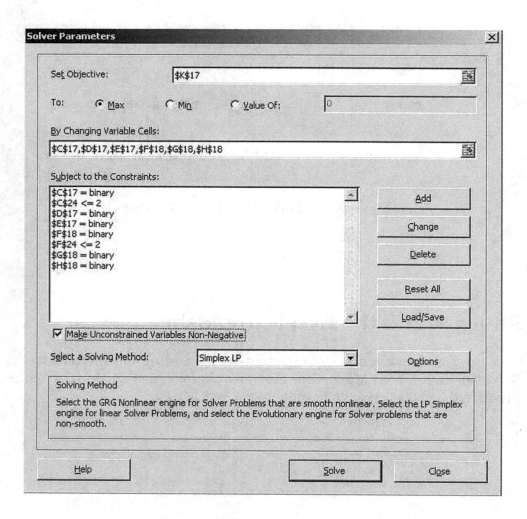

All equations on the Excel spreadsheet are linear (1st order) so we can use the Simplex LP (Linear Programming) Solver engine for this optimization problem.

Step 3 shows the completed problem with Decision Variables that have been optimized by the Solver to maximize the Objective while staying within the problem's Constraints.

Answer Report

Part 1

Note:
- The Solver Result
- How long Solver took to solve the problem
- The Solver Engine that was used and the Solver Options settings
- Where the Objective Cell was labeled in the Excel model for its name to appear as it does in Part 1 of the Answer Report

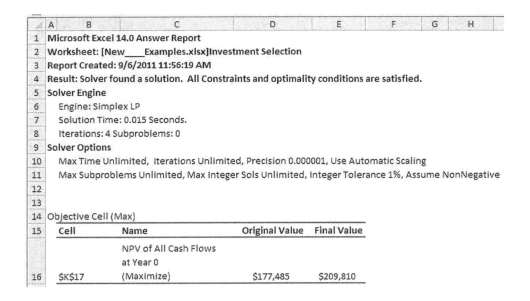

	A	B	C	D	E	F	G	H
1	Microsoft Excel 14.0 Answer Report							
2	Worksheet: [New____Examples.xlsx]Investment Selection							
3	Report Created: 9/6/2011 11:56:19 AM							
4	Result: Solver found a solution. All Constraints and optimality conditions are satisfied.							
5	Solver Engine							
6	Engine: Simplex LP							
7	Solution Time: 0.015 Seconds.							
8	Iterations: 4 Subproblems: 0							
9	Solver Options							
10	Max Time Unlimited, Iterations Unlimited, Precision 0.000001, Use Automatic Scaling							
11	Max Subproblems Unlimited, Max Integer Sols Unlimited, Integer Tolerance 1%, Assume NonNegative							
12								
13								
14	Objective Cell (Max)							
15	Cell	Name		Original Value	Final Value			
16	$K$17	NPV of All Cash Flows at Year 0 (Maximize)		$177,485	$209,810			

Part 2

- Note that the Variable Cells contain the Decision Variables
- Note where the labels for each Decision Variable are placed in the Excel model so that the Decision Variable's name will appear here in Part 2 of the Answer Report as it does
- Note the type of variable - Either Continuous or Integer (Integer, **Binary**, or Alldifferent)
- Note the Before and After values of each Decision Variable

	A	B	C	D	E	F
19	Variable Cells					
20		Cell	Name	Original Value	Final Value	Integer
21		$C$17	Year 1 Opportunity 1	1	1	Binary
22		$D$17	Year 1 Opportunity 2	1	1	Binary
23		$E$17	Year 1 Opportunity 3	1	0	Binary
24		$F$18	Year 2 Opportunity 1	1	0	Binary
25		$G$18	Year 2 Opportunity 2	1	1	Binary
26		$H$18	Year 2 Opportunity 3	1	0	Binary

Part 3

- Note how each Constraint is labeled in the Excel model in order for the Constraint's name to appear here in Part 3 of the Answer Report as it does
- Note which Constraints are binding (had their limits hit) and which aren't.
- Note how much slack is still available in any Constraint that has not had its limit hit.
- Note any Integer Constraints (Integer, Binary, Alldifferent)

	A	B	C	D	E	F	G
28							
29	Constraints						
30		Cell	Name	Cell Value	Formula	Status	Slack
31		$C$24	Total Number of Investments Made During 1st Year	2	$C$24<=2	Binding	0
32		$F$24	Total Number of Investments Made During 2nd Year	1	$F$24<=2	Not Binding	1
33		$C$17=Binary					
34		$D$17=Binary					
35		$E$17=Binary					
36		$F$18=Binary					
37		$G$18=Binary					
38		$H$18=Binary					

Supplier Shipping/Purchasing Cost Minimization

Minimize the Total Cost of Purchasing and Shipping From Multiple Suppliers

This is very similar to a previous Solver problem in this manual called Shipping Cost Reduction except that now there is variation in the purchase price of the product. Product is being purchased and then shipped from multiple sources to multiple destinations. Shipping rates for each source/destination are different, as are purchase prices from each source. Each destination requires a different amount of product and the sources all have different amounts of product available. The Objective is to minimize the total cost of purchasing and shipping.

The Problem

4 factories within 1 company obtain the same raw material Product A from 4 different outside suppliers. Each of the 4 suppliers provides a different per unit purchase price for Product A. Per unit shipping costs also vary greatly between each of the 4 suppliers and each of the 4 factories. Each of the 4 factories requires a different amount of Product A and each of the 4 suppliers has a different amount of Product A available. Determine the optimal amounts of Product A to purchase and ship between each supplier and each factory in order to minimize total purchase and shipping cost.

Specific information about the purchase price from each supplier and the shipping cost between each supplier and each factory is as follows:

	A	B	C	D	E	F	G
1							
2			Per Unit Price of Product A From Each of 4 Suppliers				
3							
4			Supplier 1	Supplier 2	Supplier 3	Supplier 4	
5			$12	$11	$11	$12	
6							
7							
8			Per Unit Shipping Cost of Product A From Each of 4 Suppliers To Factories				
9							
10			Supplier 1	Supplier 2	Supplier 3	Supplier 4	
11		Factory 1	$4	$3	$6	$3	
12		Factory 2	$7	$4	$4	$5	
13		Factory 3	$2	$5	$5	$6	
14		Factory 4	$6	$6	$8	$4	

Problem Solving Steps

Step 1 – Determine the Objective

In this case, the objective is to minimize the total cost of purchasing and shipping Product A. The cell that calculates this total cost is the Objective Cell.

Step 2 – Determine the Decision Variables

We are trying to determine how many units of Product A to purchase from each supplier and ship to each factory in order to minimize the total cost. The Decision Variables are the numbers of units of Product A purchased from each supplier that will be shipped to each factory.

Step 3 – Build the Excel Equations That Combine the Objective With All Decision Variables

	A	B	C	D	E	F	G
1							
2			Per Unit Price of Product A From Each of 4 Suppliers				
3							
4			Supplier 1	Supplier 2	Supplier 3	Supplier 4	
5			$12	$11	$11	$12	
6							
7							
8			Per Unit Shipping Cost of Product A From Each of 4 Suppliers To Factories				
9							
10			Supplier 1	Supplier 2	Supplier 3	Supplier 4	
11		Factory 1	$4	$3	$6	$3	
12		Factory 2	$7	$4	$4	$5	
13		Factory 3	$2	$5	$5	$6	
14		Factory 4	$6	$6	$8	$4	
15							
16							

	A	B	C	D	E	F	G
16							
17			Amount in Units Purchased From Each Supplier For Each Factory				
18			(Decision Variables)				
19			Units from Supplier 1	Units from Supplier 2	Units from Supplier 3	Units from Supplier 4	Total Units Received
20		Factory 1	0	5	0	15	20
21		Factory 2	0	10	20	0	30
22		Factory 3	40	0	0	0	40
23		Factory 4	0	0	0	50	50
24			Total Number of Units Purchased From Supplier A	Total Number of Units Purchased From Supplier B	Total Number of Units Purchased From Supplier C	Total Number of Units Purchased From Supplier D	Constraints
25			40	15	20	65	
			Constraint	Constraint	Constraint	Constraint	

	A	B	C	D	E	F	G
28							
29			Total Purchase Price of Product A From Each Supplier				
30			Supplier 1	Supplier 2	Supplier 3	Supplier 4	Total
31			$480	$165	$220	$780	$1,645
32							
33							
34			Total Shipping Cost of Product A From Each Supplier				
35			Supplier 1	Supplier 2	Supplier 3	Supplier 4	Total
36			$80	$55	$80	$245	$460
37							Total Cost Of Purchasing and Shipping Product A From All Suppliers To All Factories (Minimize)
38							$2,105
39							Objective
40							

The dark gray Decision Variables (C20 to F23) shown in a previous image are number of units of Product A purchased from each supplier for each factory. The medium gray Constraint cells (G20 to G23) on the right side of the model display the total number of units shipped to each factory.

The medium gray Constraint cells (C25 to F25) on the bottom of the model display the total number of units shipped from each supplier. Placing the Constraint cells here provides an efficient method to ensure that each factory receives the number of units it needs and that each supplier does not attempt to ship more units than they have available.

The total number of units shipped from each supplier and the number of units shipped from each supplier to each factory are used to used to calculate total purchase and shipping costs from all suppliers. These calculations once again are shown as follows:

	A	B	C	D	E	F	G
28							
29			Total Purchase Price of Product A From Each Supplier				
30			Supplier 1	Supplier 2	Supplier 3	Supplier 4	Total
31			$480	$165	$220	$780	$1,645
32							
33							
34			Total Shipping Cost of Product A From Each Supplier				
35			Supplier 1	Supplier 2	Supplier 3	Supplier 4	Total
36			$80	$55	$80	$245	$460
37							Total Cost Of Purchasing and Shipping Product A From All Suppliers To All Factories (Minimize)
38							$2,105
39							Objective
40							

The total cost of purchasing from all suppliers and the total cost of shipping from all suppliers is shown in the preceding image. These 2 costs are added together to create the Total Cost, which is shown in the light gray Objective cell G38.

Step 4 – List all Constraints

	B	C	D	E	F
41		Constraints			
42		20	=	Total Units Needed By Factory 1	
43					
44		30	=	Total Units Needed By Factory 2	
45					
46		40	=	Total Units Needed By Factory 3	
47					
48		50	=	Total Units Needed By Factory 4	

	B	C	D	E	F	G	H
50							
51							
52		100	=	Total Units Available From Supplier A			
53							
54		15	=	Total Units Available From Supplier B			
55							
56		20	=	Total Units Available From Supplier C			
57							
58		150	=	Total Units Available From Supplier D			
59							
60		Integer		All 16 Decision Variables (green cells)			
61				(Amount Purchased From Each Factory For Each Supplier)			
62							
63		Nonnegative		All Unconstrained Variables			

These medium gray cells are user-controlled inputs and connect with the medium gray Constraint cells in the Excel model. These user-controlled inputs determine how large each factory's order is and how many units each supplier has available to ship.

Step 5 – Test the Excel spreadsheet

Test the Excel spreadsheet completely before adding information to the Solver dialogue box. Make sure that any changes to Decision Variables produce the correct results in the Objective cell.

Step 6 – Insert All Data into the Solver Dialogue Box

Input the Objective cell, Decision Variable cell, and all Constraints into the Solver dialogue box as follows:

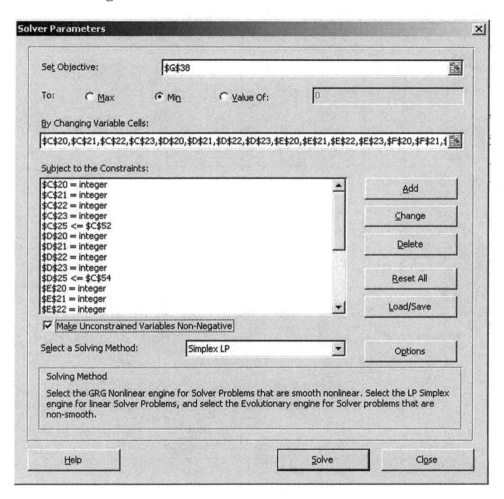

Note that the Integer Constraint must be applied to Decision Variables to ensure that only whole numbers of units are shipped. Inequality Constraints are used to limit the factories' order sizes and the suppliers' product availability.

We have to scroll the slider in the Constraints window down to see the rest of the Constraints. Here is the view of Constraints at the bottom of the list:

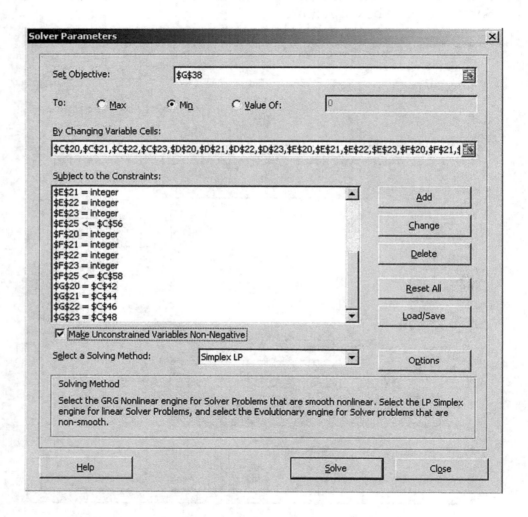

All equations on the Excel spreadsheet are linear (1st order) so we can use the Simplex LP (Linear Programming) method for this optimization problem.

Step 3 shows the completed problem with Decision Variables that have been optimized by the Solver to minimize the Objective while staying within the problem's Constraints.

Answer Report

Part 1

Note:
- The Solver Result
- How long Solver took to solve the problem
- The Solver Engine that was used and the Solver Options settings
- Where the Objective Cell was labeled in the Excel model for its name to appear as it does in Part 1 of the Answer Report

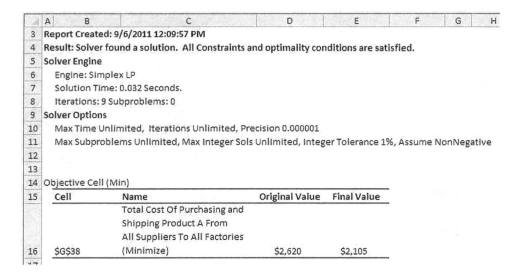

	A	B	C	D	E	F	G	H
3	Report Created: 9/6/2011 12:09:57 PM							
4	Result: Solver found a solution. All Constraints and optimality conditions are satisfied.							
5	Solver Engine							
6	Engine: Simplex LP							
7	Solution Time: 0.032 Seconds.							
8	Iterations: 9 Subproblems: 0							
9	Solver Options							
10	Max Time Unlimited, Iterations Unlimited, Precision 0.000001							
11	Max Subproblems Unlimited, Max Integer Sols Unlimited, Integer Tolerance 1%, Assume NonNegative							
12								
13								
14	Objective Cell (Min)							
15	Cell	Name		Original Value	Final Value			
16	$G$38	Total Cost Of Purchasing and Shipping Product A From All Suppliers To All Factories (Minimize)		$2,620	$2,105			

Part 2

- Note that the Variable Cells contain the Decision Variables
- Note where the labels for each Decision Variable are placed in the Excel model so that the Decision Variable's name will appear here in Part 2 of the Answer Report as it does
- Note the type of variable   - Either Continuous or Integer (**Integer**, Binary, or Alldifferent)
- Note the Before and After values of each Decision Variable

	A	B	C	D	E	F
19		Variable Cells				
20		Cell	Name	Original Value	Final Value	Integer
21		$C$20	Factory 1 Units from Supplier 1	10	0	Integer
22		$C$21	Factory 2 Units from Supplier 1	10	0	Integer
23		$C$22	Factory 3 Units from Supplier 1	10	40	Integer
24		$C$23	Factory 4 Units from Supplier 1	10	0	Integer
25		$D$20	Factory 1 Units from Supplier 2	10	5	Integer
26		$D$21	Factory 2 Units from Supplier 2	10	10	Integer
27		$D$22	Factory 3 Units from Supplier 2	10	0	Integer
28		$D$23	Factory 4 Units from Supplier 2	10	0	Integer

	A	B	C	D	E	F
28		$D$23	Factory 4 Units from Supplier 2	10	0	Integer
29		$E$20	Factory 1 Units from Supplier 3	10	0	Integer
30		$E$21	Factory 2 Units from Supplier 3	10	20	Integer
31		$E$22	Factory 3 Units from Supplier 3	10	0	Integer
32		$E$23	Factory 4 Units from Supplier 3	10	0	Integer
33		$F$20	Factory 1 Units from Supplier 4	10	15	Integer
34		$F$21	Factory 2 Units from Supplier 4	10	0	Integer
35		$F$22	Factory 3 Units from Supplier 4	10	0	Integer
36		$F$23	Factory 4 Units from Supplier 4	10	50	Integer

Part 3

- Note how each Constraint is labeled in the Excel model in order for the Constraint's name to appear here in Part 3 of the Answer Report as it does
- Note which Constraints are binding (had their limits hit) and which aren't.
- Note how much slack is still available in any Constraint that has not had its limit hit.
- Note any Integer Constraints (Integer, Binary, Alldifferent)

	A	B	C	D	E	F	G
38							
39	Constraints						
40	Cell		Name	Cell Value	Formula	Status	Slack
41	$C$25		Total Number of Units Purchased From Supplier A	40	$C$25<=$C$52	Not Binding	60
42	$D$25		Total Number of Units Purchased From Supplier B	15	$D$25<=$C$54	Binding	0
43	$E$25		Total Number of Units Purchased From Supplier C	20	$E$25<=$C$56	Binding	0
44	$F$25		Total Number of Units Purchased From Supplier D	65	$F$25<=$C$58	Not Binding	85
45	$G$20		Factory 1 Total Units Received	20	$G$20=$C$42	Binding	0
46	$G$21		Factory 2 Total Units Received	30	$G$21=$C$44	Binding	0
47	$G$22		Factory 3 Total Units Received	40	$G$22=$C$46	Binding	0
48	$G$23		Factory 4 Total Units Received	50	$G$23=$C$48	Binding	0

	A	B	C	D	E	F	G
47		$G$22	Factory 3 Total Units Received	40	$G$22=$C$46	Binding	0
48		$G$23	Factory 4 Total Units Received	50	$G$23=$C$48	Binding	0
49		$C$20=Integer					
50		$C$21=Integer					
51		$C$22=Integer					
52		$C$23=Integer					
53		$D$20=Integer					
54		$D$21=Integer					
55		$D$22=Integer					
56		$D$23=Integer					
57		$E$20=Integer					
58		$E$21=Integer					
59		$E$22=Integer					
60		$E$23=Integer					
61		$F$20=Integer					
62		$F$21=Integer					
63		$F$22=Integer					
64		$F$23=Integer					

Traveling Salesman Problem

Using the Alldifferent Constraint and the Evolutionary Method To Select the Shortest Path That Reaches All Customers

This is a classic Solver problem that provides a great opportunity to illustrate the use of the Alldifferent Constraint and the Evolutionary Solver. A traveling salesman must visit a given number of customers and pick the shortest path that will reach every customer and bring him back to his starting point.

The **Alldifferent Constraint** is used to ensure that the salesman visits each customer only once. The **Evolutionary method** is used because the mathematical path to the Objective contains the Excel Index lookup function, which is a discontinuous function.

The Problem

A traveling salesman living in Chicago must make stops in these 4 other cities: LA, Denver, Boston, and Dallas. He must start and finish in his home city of Chicago. He must select the order of customers to visit that will minimize the total length of the trip.

Below is the specific information about the distances between each of the 5 cities:

	A	B	C	D	E	F	G
1		Distances Between Cities					
2			Boston	Chicago	Dallas	Denver	LA
3		Boston	0	983	1815	1991	3036
4		Chicago	983	0	1205	1050	2112
5		Dallas	1815	1205	0	801	1425
6		Denver	1991	1050	801	0	1174
7		LA	3036	2112	1425	1174	0

Problem Solving Steps

Step 1 – Determine the Objective

In this case, the objective is to minimize the total distance traveled when traveling between all 5 cities. The total distance traveled by the salesman is the Objective to be minimized.

Step 2 – Determine the Decision Variables

We are trying to select the order of cities to visit that minimizes the total distance travelled. The cities are designated in the Excel model not by their names but by the row that they appear in the distance chart just shown.

Boston appears in the 1st row of the distance chart. Boston is therefore designated with a "1." Chicago appears in the 2nd row in the chart and is therefore assigned a designation of "2." Dallas appears in the 3rd row and is designated "3." Denver appears in the 4th row and is designated "4." LA appears in the 5th row and is designated "5."

We need to determine the order of cities to visit to minimize the total miles travelled. In other words, we are minimizing the sum of distances travelled between consecutive cities.

Step 3 – Build the Excel Equations That Combine the Objective With All Decision Variables

A	B	C	D	E	F	G	H	I
8			City In The Row (Uses the Index Function To Lookup That City)					
9	Actual Trip Order	City Row In Chart		Distance From Previous City				
10	1st City Visted	1	Boston	3036	=INDEX(C3:G7,C10,C14)			
11	2nd City Visted	2	Chicago	983	=INDEX($C$3:$G$7,C10,C11)			
12	3rd City Visted	3	Dallas	1205	=INDEX($C$3:$G$7,C11,C12)			
13	4th City Visted	4	Denver	801	=INDEX($C$3:$G$7,C12,C13)			
14	5th City Visted	5	LA	1174	=INDEX($C$3:$G$7,C13,C14)			
15		Decision Variables (The Alldifferent Constraint Is Applied To All)		Total Miles (Minimize)				
16				7199				
17				Objective				

Column C – Decision Variables

The Decision Variables are the arrangement of the cities to visit. In the preceding diagram, the Decision Variables are the row designations of each city. These Decision Variables are in cells C10 to C14. The order of the Decision Variables shown above (1, 2, 3, 4, 5) indicate that the cities will be visited in this order: Boston (row 1 in the Distance Chart) to Chicago (row 2 in the Distance Chart) to Dallas (row 3 in the Distance Chart) to Denver (row 4 in the Distance Chart) to LA (row 5 in the Distance Chart) and back to Boston.

This set of 5 Decision Variables are collectively subject to the Alldifferent Constraint. As a result, each 1 of these 5 Decision Variables will be assigned an integer between 1 and 5. None of the 5 Decision Variables in this set can be assigned the same number.

Column D – Listing The Cities Attached To Decision Variables

The Excel Index function is used in column D to list the city which corresponds to the Distance Chart row number that appears in column C. For example, cell D10 contains the Excel formula:

=INDEX($B$3:$B$7,$C10,1).

The Index function has the following syntax:

=INDEX(range, row number, column number)

For the above formula, the range is the cells from B3 to B7. This is a range of cells that has only 1 column.

The row number referenced in this Index function is in cell C10. The contents of Cell C10 = 1. The row referenced by this Index function is the 1st row.

The column number referenced in this Index function is 1. This would have to be the case since only 1 column exists within the given range (B3 to B7).

The Index function displays the contents of the cell in the given row (1st row) and column (1st column) of the given range. This Index function will display the contents of the cell in the 1st row and the 1st column of the given range (B3 to B7). The cell in the 1st row and the 1st column of cell range (B3 to B7) is cell B3. Cell B3 contains the word Boston, which is displayed in cell D10.

Column E – Calculating Distances Between Each City and the Previously Visited City

The distances between each city and the previous city visited are shown to the right in column E. For example, the distance between Boston and the previous city of LA is 3036 miles. The distance between Chicago and the previous city of Boston is 983 miles. The distance between Dallas and the previous city of Chicago is 1205 miles. The distance between Denver and the previous city of Dallas is 801 miles. The distance between LA and the previous city of Denver is 1174.

Distances between each city and its previous city are found by using the Index function. This function looks up in the Distances chart and locates and displays the distance between a city and its previously visited city.

The distances shown in Column E are as follows:

The distance between Boston and the previous city of LA is 3036 miles.

The distance between Chicago and the previous city of Boston is 983 miles.

The distance between Dallas and the previous city of Chicago is 1205 miles.

The distance between Denver and the previous city of Dallas is 801 miles.

The distance between LA and the previous city of Denver is 1174.

The Excel Index functions which generated each of these distances are shown to the right of each distance. An explanation of this use of the Index function is as follows:

The Index function has the following syntax:

=INDEX(range, row number, column number)

For the above formula, the range is the cells from C3 to G7. This cell range holds the distances in the Distance Chart.

The row number corresponds to the previous city visited. This row number is the previous city's row number in the Distance chart.

The column number corresponds to the current city. This column number is the current city's column number in the Distance chart.

All of the distances between cities are listed in cells C3 to G7. The Index function locates the cell that holds the distance between each city and the previous city. Each distance will be found in the row number of the that previous city and column number of the current city.

The order of the cities (actually, the order of the city row numbers in column C) are arranged so that sum of the distances between each city and the previous city is minimized.

Step 4 – List all Constraints

This problem provides an excellent opportunity to showcase the Alldifferent Constraint. We are visiting each city only once so we need each city (actually the city's row number in the Distance Chart) to be listed only one time without repeating.

Each city's unique row number in the Distance Chart must be assigned to only 1 of the 5 Decision Variable cells. We must therefore apply the Alldifferent Constraint to all of the Decision Variable cells (cells C10 to C14) simultaneously as a group. As a result of the Alldifferent Constraint, these 5 cells will hold the integers 1 to 5. No 2 cells in this group will be assigned the same number. This ensures that each city will be visited only once and that all cities will be visited.

The following Solver Dialogue box shows the set of 5 Decision Variables (Cells C10 to C14) subject collectively to the Alldifferent Constraint.

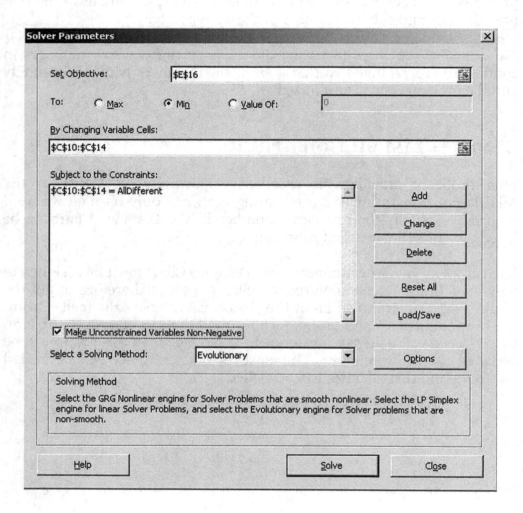

Step 5 – Test the Excel Spreadsheet

This spreadsheet can be very easily tested by varying the integer values in the Decision Variable cells (cells C10 to C14). The city names and distances between cities should correctly change to match the new Decision Variable integer values corresponding to different rows.

Step 6 – Insert All Data into the Solver Dialogue Box

Once again here is the completed Solver dialogue box:

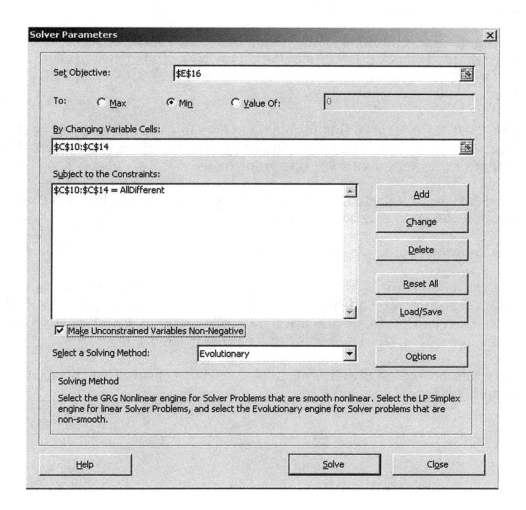

The Travelling Salesman Problem provides an excellent opportunity to demonstrate the use of the Evolutionary method. The Evolutionary method must be used if the Mathematical Path to the Objective contains any cells holding non-smooth or discontinuous formulas.

Common non-smooth Excel functions are MIN, MAX, and ABS.

Common discontinuous Excel functions are **INDEX**, HLOOKUP, VLOOKUP, LOOKUP, INT, ROUND, COUNT, CEILING, FLOOR, IF, CHOOSE, NOT AND, OR, GREATER THAN, LESS THAN, and EQUAL TO.

The INDEX function in this problem appears in cells that are part of the Clear Mathematical Path to the Objective. We therefore must select the Evolutionary method to solve this problem.

After we have selected the Evolutionary method, we hit Solve and solution shown in several pages is reached.

This solution could be interpreted as follows:

The salesman stars in his home town of Chicago. He then visits Denver, LA, Dallas, Boston, and finally back to Chicago in that order. The total miles travelled on this route are 6,447 miles. This is the shortest route that will cover all 5 cities starting and ending in Chicago.

Note that no special provision has to be made to ensure that the starting point is Chicago.

Following are views of the Excel model before solving and then after solving with Excel Solver's Evolutionary method:

Before Running Solver

	A	B	C	D	E	F	G	H	I
8				City in The Row (Uses the Index Function To Lookup That City)					
9			Actual Trip Order	City Row In Chart		Distance From Previous City				
10			1st City Visted	1	Boston	3036	=INDEX(C3:G7,C10,C14)			
11			2nd City Visted	2	Chicago	983	=INDEX($C$3:$G$7,C10,C11)			
12			3rd City Visted	3	Dallas	1205	=INDEX($C$3:$G$7,C11,C12)			
13			4th City Visted	4	Denver	801	=INDEX($C$3:$G$7,C12,C13)			
14			5th City Visted	5	LA	1174	=INDEX($C$3:$G$7,C13,C14)			
15				Decision Variables (The Alldifferent Constraint Is Applied To All)		Total Miles (Minimize)				
16						7199				
17						Objective				

After Running Solver

	Actual Trip Order	City Row In Chart	City in The Row (Uses the Index Function To Lookup That City)	Distance From Previous City	
1st City Visted		5	LA	1425	=INDEX(C3:G7,C10,C14)
2nd City Visted		4	Denver	1174	=INDEX($C$3:$G$7,C10,C11)
3rd City Visted		2	Chicago	1050	=INDEX($C$3:$G$7,C11,C12)
4th City Visted		1	Boston	983	=INDEX($C$3:$G$7,C12,C13)
5th City Visted		3	Dallas	1815	=INDEX($C$3:$G$7,C13,C14)
		Decision Variables (The Alldifferent Constraint Is Applied To All)		Total Miles (Minimize)	
				6447	
				Objective	

	Actual Trip Order	City Row In Chart	City in The Row (Uses the Index Function To Lookup That City)	Distance From Previous City		
1st City Visted	5	LA	1425	=INDEX(C3:G7,C10,C14)		
2nd City Visted	4	Denver	1174	=INDEX($C$3:$G$7,C10,C11)		
3rd City Visted	2	Chicago	1050	=INDEX($C$3:$G$7,C11,C12)		
4th City Visted	1	Boston	983	=INDEX($C$3:$G$7,C12,C13)		
5th City Visted	3	Dallas	1815	=INDEX($C$3:$G$7,C13,C14)		
	Decision Variables (The Alldifferent Constraint Is Applied To All)		Total Miles (Minimize)			
			6447			
			Objective			

Answer Report

Part 1

Note:
- The Solver Result
- **How long Solver took to solve the problem** (especially important in this case – This time could be reduced by several of the Options settings.)
- The Solver Engine that was used and the Solver Options settings
- Where the Objective Cell was labeled in the Excel model for its name to appear as it does in Part 1 of the Answer Report

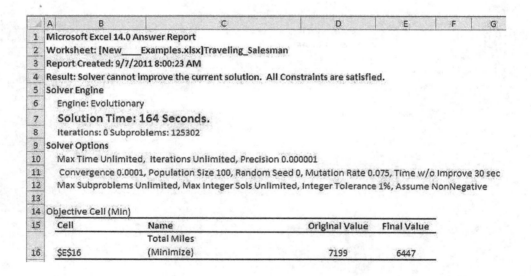

	A	B	C	D	E	F	G
1	Microsoft Excel 14.0 Answer Report						
2	Worksheet: [New____Examples.xlsx]Traveling_Salesman						
3	Report Created: 9/7/2011 8:00:23 AM						
4	Result: Solver cannot improve the current solution. All Constraints are satisfied.						
5	Solver Engine						
6	Engine: Evolutionary						
7	**Solution Time: 164 Seconds.**						
8	Iterations: 0 Subproblems: 125302						
9	Solver Options						
10	Max Time Unlimited, Iterations Unlimited, Precision 0.000001						
11	Convergence 0.0001, Population Size 100, Random Seed 0, Mutation Rate 0.075, Time w/o Improve 30 sec						
12	Max Subproblems Unlimited, Max Integer Sols Unlimited, Integer Tolerance 1%, Assume NonNegative						
13							
14	Objective Cell (Min)						
15	Cell	Name		Original Value	Final Value		
16	$E$16	Total Miles (Minimize)		7199	6447		

Note the solution time of 164 seconds. This could have been reduced by limiting the maximum allowable run time, iterations, or subproblems using the Options menu.

Part 2 – Variable Cells

- Note that the Variable Cells contain the Decision Variables
- Note where the labels for each Decision Variable are placed in the Excel model so that the Decision Variable's name will appear here in Part 2 of the Answer Report as it does
- Note the type of variable - Either Continuous or Integer (Integer, Binary, or **Alldifferent**)
- Note the Before and After values of each Decision Variable

Part 3 - Constraints

- Note how each Constraint is labeled in the Excel model in order for the Constraint's name to appear here in Part 3 of the Answer Report as it does
- Note which Constraints are binding (had their limits hit) and which aren't.
- Note how much slack is still available in any Constraint that has not had its limit hit.
- Note any Integer Constraints (Integer, Binary, Alldifferent)

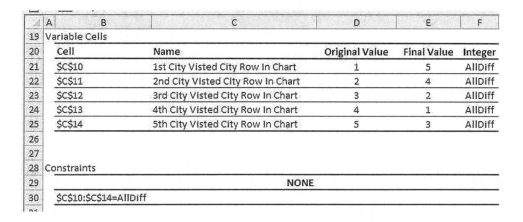

	Cell	Name	Original Value	Final Value	Integer
19	Variable Cells				
20	Cell	Name	Original Value	Final Value	Integer
21	$C$10	1st City Visted City Row In Chart	1	5	AllDiff
22	$C$11	2nd City Visted City Row In Chart	2	4	AllDiff
23	$C$12	3rd City Visted City Row In Chart	3	2	AllDiff
24	$C$13	4th City Visted City Row In Chart	4	1	AllDiff
25	$C$14	5th City Visted City Row In Chart	5	3	AllDiff
26					
27					
28	Constraints				
29		NONE			
30	$C$10:$C$14=AllDiff				

Note that Cells C10 to C14 were set to AllDiff simultaneously as a group.

Population Report

The Population Report is made available when the Evolutionary method is used. The Population Report provides indication about whether and how you can make improvements to the model or to the Evolutionary method Options

The Population Report can be valuable if successive runs of the Evolutionary method produce different answers for the Objective. The setting of the Mean Value and Standard Deviation during successive runs provide insight into whether your successive solutions are getting closer to the most optimal solution. See the section on a detail description of this report for more information about this topic.

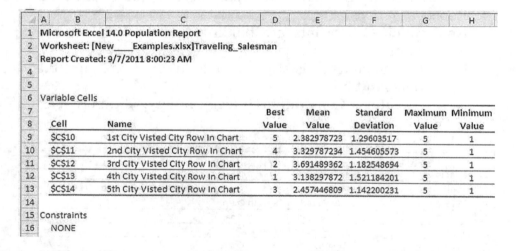

	A	B	C	D	E	F	G	H
1	Microsoft Excel 14.0 Population Report							
2	Worksheet: [New____Examples.xlsx]Traveling_Salesman							
3	Report Created: 9/7/2011 8:00:23 AM							
4								
5								
6	Variable Cells							
7				Best	Mean	Standard	Maximum	Minimum
8		Cell	Name	Value	Value	Deviation	Value	Value
9		$C$10	1st City Visted City Row In Chart	5	2.382978723	1.29603517	5	1
10		$C$11	2nd City Visted City Row In Chart	4	3.329787234	1.454605573	5	1
11		$C$12	3rd City Visted City Row In Chart	2	3.691489362	1.182548694	5	1
12		$C$13	4th City Visted City Row In Chart	1	3.138297872	1.521184201	5	1
13		$C$14	5th City Visted City Row In Chart	3	2.457446809	1.142200231	5	1
14								
15	Constraints							
16	NONE							

How To Perform Nonlinear Regression

Perform Nonlinear Regression and Curve Fitting Using the GRG Nonlinear Method

Excel Solver is one of the best and easiest curve-fitting devices in the world, if you know how to use it as such. Its curve-fitting capabilities make it an excellent tool for performing nonlinear regression. The Excel Solver can be used to find the equation of the linear or nonlinear curve which most closely fits a set of data points.

One very important caveat must be added: the user must first visually determine the most likely type of the curve that will fit the data and then input that information into Solver at the start. This information is in the form of the general equation that defines the curve, such as $a_0 + a_1 * x + a_2 * x^2 = c$ or $a * \ln(x^b) = c$. Solver then calculates the values of all needed variables which produce the equation that most closely fits the data points. We will run through an example here.

In this problem we are going to show how to use the Excel Solver to calculate an equation which most closely describes the relationship between sales and number of ads being run. The purpose of this equation is to create an equation that will most accurately predict the number of sales given the number of ads that have just been run.

We will then graph the actual and predicted data points. This will illustrate that nonlinear regression and curve fitting are almost the same thing.

A marketing manager has collected this following data on the company's sales vs. the number of ads that were running in the week prior to collecting each sales data point.

Sales Number of Ads Running

Sales	Number of Ads Running
50	6700
55	7500
59	8700
62	8900
75	8800
95	10900
110	11200
125	11400
140	11500
180	12300

Here is an Excel scatter plot of this actual sales data:

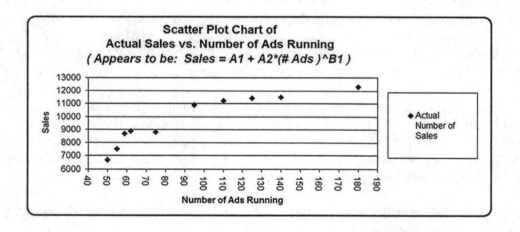

We would like to create an equation from this data that will allow us to predict the sales based upon the number of ads run in the previous week.

The first step is to eyeball the data and estimate what general type of curve these data points most likely fit to. In this case the data points appear to a graph the has a diminishing y value for an increasing x value. The formula for such a curve would have this general form:

$$Y = A_1 + A_2 * X^{B_1}$$

$$Sales = A_1 + A_2 * (Number\ of\ Ads\ Running)^{B_1}$$

We can use the Excel Solver to solve for A1, A2, and B1. We need to arrange the data in this format as inputs into the Excel Solver as follows:

	A	B	C	D	E	F	G
1							
2			Number of Ads Running	Actual Number of Sales	Predicted Number of Sales By Model	Difference	Square of Difference
3	A1	-445616	50	6,700	7,495	-795	631,435
4	A2	437246.9	55	7,500	7,888	-388	150,725
5	B1	0.00911	59	8,700	8,178	522	272,092
6		Decision	62	8,900	8,383	517	266,810
7		Variables	75	8,800	9,171	-371	137,978
8			95	10,900	10,152	748	559,629
9			110	11,200	10,761	439	192,686
10			125	11,400	11,293	107	11,483
11			140	11,500	11,765	-265	70,129
12			180	12,300	12,813	-513	263,377
13							Sum of Squared Differenced
14							2,556,343
15							Objective

The preceding image shows the Excel model after it has already been solved. By "solved," we mean in this case that the Solver has calculated the Decision Variable values (in the dark gray cells B3 to B5) that minimize the Objective.

	A	B	C	D	E	F	G
2			Number of Ads Running	Actual Number of Sales	Predicted Number of Sales By Model	Difference	Square of Difference
3	A1	-445616	50	6,700	7,495	-795	631,435
4	A2	457246.9	55	7,500	7,888	-388	150,725
5	B1	0.00911	59	8,700	8,178	522	272,092
6		Decision	62	8,900	8,383	517	266,810
7		Variables	75	8,800	9,171	-371	137,978
8			95	10,900	10,152	748	559,629
9			110	11,200	10,761	439	192,686
10			125	11,400	11,293	107	11,483
11			140	11,500	11,765	-265	70,129
12			180	12,300	12,813	-513	263,377
13							Sum of Squared Differenced
14							2,556,343
15							Objective

	A	B	C	D	E	F	G
7		Variables	75	8,800	9,171	-371	137,978
8			95	10,900	10,152	748	559,629
9			110	11,200	10,761	439	192,686
10			125	11,400	11,293	107	11,483
11			140	11,500	11,765	-265	70,129
12			180	12,300	12,813	-513	263,377
13							Sum of Squared Differenced
14							2,556,343
15							Objective
16							
17				E12 =$B$3+$B$4*(C12^$B$5)			
18							
19				Sales = A1 + A2*(Number of Ads Running)^{B1}			

This table shows the arrangement of data and the calculations. Here we have created an Excel model based upon our model of:

Sales = A1 + A2 * (Number of Ads Running)^{B1}

One example of this formula in action is explained for Cell E12. We are listing the variable that we are solving for (A1, A2, and B1) in cells B3 to B5. In Solver language, these solves that we are changing are called Decision Variables.

We arbitrarily set our Decision Variables for:

A1 = 100
A2 = 100
B1 = 0.05

The Excel model shown before running the Solver as follows:

Before Running Solver

	A	B	C	D	E	F	G
1							
2			Number of Ads Running	Actual Number of Sales	Predicted Number of Sales By Model	Difference	Square of Difference
3	A1	100	50	6,700	222	6,478	41,969,612
4	A2	100	55	7,500	222	7,278	52,966,590
5	B1	0.05	59	8,700	223	8,477	71,866,061
6		Decision	62	8,900	223	8,677	75,291,732
7		Variables	75	8,800	224	8,576	73,546,153
8			95	10,900	226	10,674	113,943,454
9			110	11,200	226	10,974	120,417,836
10			125	11,400	227	11,173	124,829,113
11			140	11,500	228	11,272	127,057,343
12			180	12,300	230	12,070	145,693,413
13							Sum of Squared Differenced
14							947,581,308
15							Objective

We now take the difference between the actual number of sales and the number of sales predicted by our model with our arbitrary settings for the Decision Variables. The square of each difference is taken and then all squares are summed up in the light gray Objective Cell C14.

We are trying to find the settings for the Decision Variables that will minimize the sum of the squares of the differences. In other words, we are trying to find A1, A2, and B1 that will minimize the number in cell G14.

Bring up the Excel Solver and the following blank Solver dialogue box comes up:

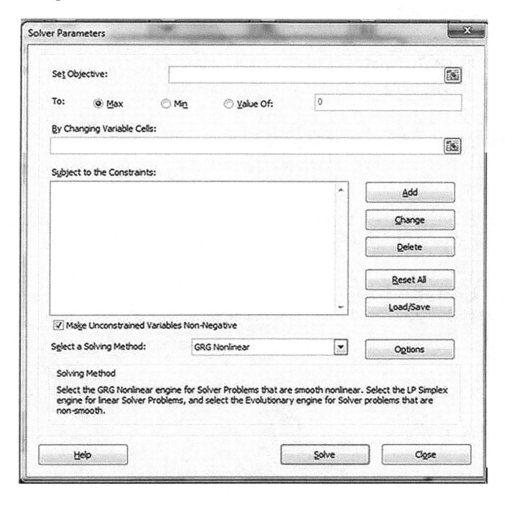

The Solver dialogue box has the following 4 parameters that need to be set:

1) The Objective Cell – This is the target cell that we are either trying to maximize, minimize, or achieve a certain value.

2) Minimize or Maximize the Target, or attempt to achieve a certain value in the Objective cell.

3) Decision Variables – A set of variables that will be changed by the Excel Solver in order to optimize the target cell.

4) Constraints – These are the limitations that the problem subjects the Solver to during its calculations

Once again, here is the data table for Solver inputs as follows:

	A	B	C	D	E	F	G
1							
2			Number of Ads Running	Actual Number of Sales	Predicted Number of Sales By Model	Difference	Square of Difference
3	A1	100	50	6,700	222	6,478	41,969,612
4	A2	100	55	7,500	222	7,278	52,966,590
5	B1	0.05	59	8,700	223	8,477	71,866,061
6		Decision	62	8,900	223	8,677	75,291,732
7		Variables	75	8,800	224	8,576	73,546,153
8			95	10,900	226	10,674	113,943,454
9			110	11,200	226	10,974	120,417,836
10			125	11,400	227	11,173	124,829,113
11			140	11,500	228	11,272	127,057,343
12			180	12,300	230	12,070	145,693,413
13							Sum of Squared Differenced
14							947,581,308
15							Objective

Objective:

We are trying to minimize light gray Objective Cell G14, the sum of the square of differences between the actual and predicted sales.

Decision Variables:

We are changing A1, A2, and B1 (dark gray cells B3 to B5) to minimize the Objective Cell G14. The Decision Variables are therefore Cells B3 to B5.

Constraints:

There are none for this curve-fitting operation.

Selection of Solving Method: GRG Nonlinear

The GRG Nonlinear method is used when the equation producing the objective is not linear but is smooth (continuous). Examples of smooth nonlinear functions in Excel are:

=1/C1, =Log(C1), and =C1^2

These functions have graphs that are curved (nonlinear), but have no breaks (smooth)

Our sales equation appears to be smooth and non-linear:

Sales = A1 + A2 * (Number of Ads Running)^{B1}

The completed Solver dialogue box:

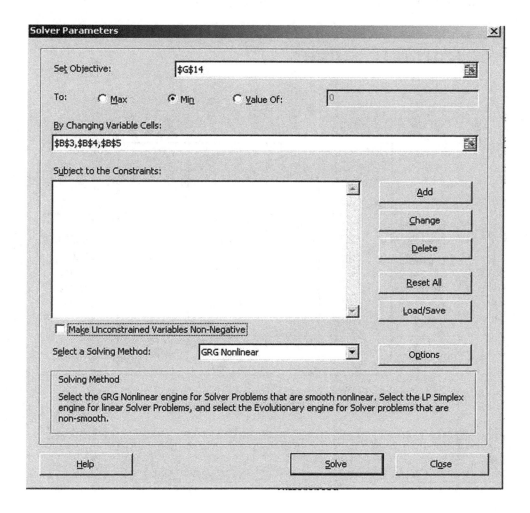

Note that we do not want to check the option **Make Unconstrained Variables Non-Negative**. It is possible that coefficients of the regression equation will be negative. It turns out that 1 of the regression coefficients actually is negative.

If we now hit the Solve button, we get the following result, which in this case is the set of Decision Variables that minimize the Objective:

After Running Solver

	A	B	C	D	E	F	G
1							
2			Number of Ads Running	Actual Number of Sales	Predicted Number of Sales By Model	Difference	Square of Difference
3	A1	-445616	50	6,700	7,495	-795	631,435
4	A2	437246.9	55	7,500	7,888	-388	150,725
5	B1	0.00911	59	8,700	8,178	522	272,092
6		Decision	62	8,900	8,383	517	266,810
7		Variables	75	8,800	9,171	-371	137,978
8			95	10,900	10,152	748	559,629
9			110	11,200	10,761	439	192,686
10			125	11,400	11,293	107	11,483
11			140	11,500	11,765	-265	70,129
12			180	12,300	12,813	-513	263,377
13							Sum of Squared Differenced
14							2,556,343
15							Objective

We actually ran Solver twice to obtain this result. Often the GRG Nonlinear method will produce different solutions on successive Solver runs. The result of each run GRG Nonlinear run on a nonlinear problem depends on the "starting point" that the Solver selects. It is often a good idea to run the GRG Nonlinear method several times in a row to find the most optimal solution.

Solver has optimized the Decision Variables to minimize the objective function as follows:

Decision Variables

A1 = -445,616
A2 = 437,247.9
B1 = 0.00911

The Objective is minimized to: 2,556,343

Solver calculates that Sales can be predicted from Number of Ads Running by the following equation:

Sales = A1 + A2 * (Number of Ads Running)^{B1}

Sales = -445616 + 437247 * (Number of Ads Running)$^{0.00911}$

We can now create an Excel graph of the Actual Sales vs. the Predicted Sales as follows:

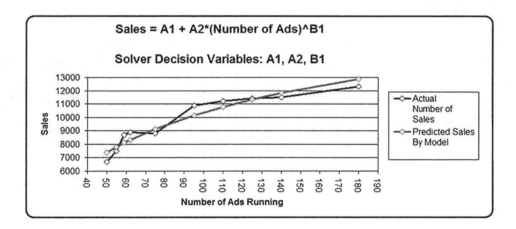

The trickiest part of this problem is the first step; eyeballing the data to determine what kind of graph the data is

arranged in. You should take time to evaluate whether you are pursuing calculation of the correct curve type.

Solver Tips

You may notice that if you run this problem through the Solver multiple time, you will get slightly different answers. Each time that you run Solver's GRG algorithm, it will calculate different values for the Decision Variables. You are trying to find the values for the Decision Variables that minimize the objective function (cell G14) the most.

When the Solver runs the GRG algorithm, it picks a starting point for its calculations. Each time you run the Solver GRG method a slightly different starting point will be picked. That is why different answers will appear during each run. Choose the Decision Variable value that occurs during the run which produces the lowest value of the Objective. Keep running the Solver until the objective is not minimized anymore. That should give you the optimal values of the Decision Variables. That was done in the example above.

Summary

Excel Solver is an easy-to-use and powerful nonlinear regression tool as a result of its curve-fitting capacity. One use of this is to calculate predictive sales equations for your company. It will work as long as you have properly determined the correct general curve type in the beginning.

When You Need A More Powerful Optimization Tool Than the Excel Solver

The Excel Solver was originally developed many years ago by Frontline Systems, Inc. in the town of Incline Village, Nevada on the scenic north shore of Lake Tahoe. Frontline Systems is still the developer of the Solver for Excel and remains headquartered in Incline Village today.

Frontline Systems developed the first Excel Solver and they have been building much more powerful Solvers and optimization tools ever since. They are the current world leaders in cutting-edge optimization software development.

The Excel Solver is an excellent and convenient tool to learn optimization. The Excel Solver does however have limitations that can be overcome only by using a more powerful Solver.

For example, one of the major limitations of the Excel Solver is the number of Decision Variables or Constraints that it can handle. The Excel Solver cannot process more than 200 Decision Variables at once. The GRG Nonlinear and Evolutionary solving methods used by the Excel Solver cannot process more than 100 constraints in additional to upper and lower bounds for variables.

It is, however, not uncommon for industrial optimization problems to contain thousands or millions of variables.

If you believe that your optimization problem will require a more powerful optimization tool than the Excel Solver, Frontline Systems is a good place to start your search. Their web site is:

http://www.solver.com

Meet Mark the Author

Mark Harmon is a master number cruncher. Creating overloaded Excel spreadsheets loaded with complicated statistical analysis is his idea of a good time. His profession as an Internet marketing manager provides him with the opportunity and the need to perform plenty of meaningful statistical analysis.

Mark Harmon is also a natural teacher. As an adjunct professor, he spent five years teaching more than thirty semester-long courses in marketing and finance at the Anglo-American College in Prague, Czech Republic and the International University in Vienna, Austria. During that five-year time period, he also worked as an independent marketing consultant in Czechoslovakia and then the Czech Republic and performed long-term assignments for more than one hundred clients. His years of teaching and consulting have honed his ability to present difficult subject matter in an easy-to-understand way.

Mark Harmon received a degree in electrical engineering from Villanova University and MBA in marketing from the Wharton School.

Check Out the Latest Manual

If You Liked
Step-By-Step Optimization With Excel Solver

You'll Love
Practical and Clear Graduate Statistics in Excel

Find Out What's In It On The Next Page

If You Wish To Purchase It, Go To:

http://www.amazon.com/dp/B004SUR6H8

Here's What's Inside
Practical and Clear Graduate Statistics In Excel

Complete and practical yet easy-to-understand graduate-level statistics course with all of the problems worked out in Excel. Thoroughly covers all topics of an intense graduate statistics course using nothing but step-by-step, simple explanations.

Loaded with completed, real-world problems all in Excel, this manual is an outstanding supplement to a graduate statistics course. Very clear explanations are used to show exactly how the Excel formulas integrate with the statistical frameworks being applied.

The reader will learn how to master and apply graduate-level statistics much faster than a student in a normal graduate statistics course because this manual's emphasis is entirely on problem solving, not on useless, forgettable theory that fills up many statistics courses.

This manual achieves two goals: teaching graduate-level statistical frameworks in an easy-to-understand way and then showing how to implement all of it in Excel.

The widely-used Microsoft Excel program provides a very simple but incredibly complete platform to perform heavy-duty, advanced statistical analysis. All other statistical software packages, such as Minitab, SyStat, and SPSS, are expensive, require lots of user training, and expect that the user is an expert statistician right from the start. Not this manual nor Microsoft Excel.

The ability to perform graduate-level statistics in Excel is an extremely useful and powerful tool for any graduate statistics student and business manager.

The statistics student will greatly appreciate never again having to look up and figure out complicated statistical charts. Homework assignments can be quickly checked with Excel. Once difficult statistical business problems are now readily solvable in Excel.

The easy-to-follow frameworks in this manual can be cleanly and swiftly duplicated in the real world and on statistics exams by hand (without Excel) right away.

The lessons are all in bite-size chunks that are quickly absorbed for immediate use. More than half of the lessons in this manual are supplemented with step-by-step videos for more convenient learning.

Some of the major topics covered in detail include regression, ANOVA, hypothesis tests, confidence intervals, combinations, permutations, correlation, covariance, t-tests, histograms, and charting.

The following distributions are explained with real-world applications using lots of solved problems: Normal distribution, t distribution, Binomial distribution, f distribution, Chi-Square distribution, Weibull distribution, Poisson distribution, Exponential distribution, Uniform distribution, Beta distribution, Gamma distribution, Hypergeometric distribution, and Multinomial distribution.

This manual also contains two complete chapters with numerous videos showing exactly how to create user-interactive graphs of the above distributions in Excel. These user-interactive Excel graphs allow the user to vary the cells containing all of the distribution's parameters, such as mean, standard deviation, and degrees of freedom, and watch the graphed distribution instantly change right on the spreadsheet to conform to the new parameters. This is an excellent and unique tool to fully grasp the functionality of the distributions discussed in this e-manual.

All problem-solving techniques are presented as step-by-step frameworks that can be readily applied to similar problems, not as seemingly unrelated and difficult-to-apply statistical theorems like most statistics course do.

A number of problem-solving techniques are presented in this manual that do not appear in any other statistical text. One example of a statistical technique presented only in this manual and nowhere else is a detailed description showing how to solve every type of hypothesis test using the same four steps.

A number of widely-used and complicated statistical tests, such as the chi-square independence test, the chi-square population variance test, and conjoint analysis using dummy variable regression are described from top to bottom and also in Excel.

Graduate statistics students and business managers will find this manual to be, by far, the easiest and fastest way to master graduate-level statistics and to apply advanced statistics in Excel to solve difficult, real-world problems, homework assignments, and exam questions.

The reader of this manual will quickly become an Excel Statistical Master.

Find Out What Readers Are Saying About Practical and Clear Graduate Statistics In Excel On The Next Page

If You Wish To Purchase It, Go To:

http://www.amazon.com/dp/B004SUR6H8

Here's What Readers Are Saying About
Practical and Clear Graduate Statistics In Excel
The Excel Statistical Master

"I bought Mark Harmon's Excel Master Series manual as a reference for a graduate course on statistics that I was taking as part of an MBA program at the University of Delaware. I purchased the materials about halfway through the course and wish I had known about this manual from the start of the class!

Mark has done a great job in writing complex statistical concepts in an easy to understand format that makes grasping them both easy to understand and to use.

With the help of Mark's book, and some diligent studying, I received an A in my stats course.

Thanks Mark!"

Chris Veale
Newark, Delaware

"The Excel Statistical Master really saved me in my graduate statistics class last semester. The book that was used in the class really did not give the practical down to earth instructions I needed to apply my statistical knowledge to excel.

In this quide I was able to find helpful step by step instructions (and pictures) that walked me through creating ANOVA's, Hypothesis testing, and so much more.

I highly recommend this book for graduate students and managers who are looking to maximize the power of Excel in their daily operational activities."

Christopher M. Walden
Jacksonville Beach, Florida

"Mark, Thanks for your invaluable material. I have used it in my current business research methods for my bachelor students. It has enabled me to abandon SPSS for the first time!

I have also given your link to <u>the last MBA class I taught. They told me that your book was of great help to understand my course!</u>"

Professor Emmanuel Fragnière
HEG Geneva and University of Bath

"After years of searching for a simplified statistics book, I found the Excel Statistical Master.

Unlike the indecipherable jargon in the countless books I have wasted money on, <u>the language in this book is plain and easy to understand.</u>

<u>This is the best $40 I have ever spent.</u>"

Mahdi Raghfar
New York, New York

"I am a medical student at Semmelweis University and <u>the Excel Statistical Master helped me so much with passing my midterms and my semifinal exam. There is no way I would have passed without it.</u>

Even though I went to all of the classes and consultations, it was the Excel Statistical Master that taught me all of the basic concepts for the different tests we used.

Each test is explained in different steps and how you performed it on Excel. Illustrations and screenshots make it <u>easy to follow, even for those like me that never had used Excel before.</u>

I highly recommend Excel Statistical Master for all medical students. It's worth every dollar. And I have to say that the communication with the seller have been the best! If I had questions about statistics problems, he more than gladly answered them. It's so easy and saved my from hours with reading!

Thanks a lot!"

Annette Myhre
Medical Student
Semmelweis University
Budapest, Hungary

"I am taking evening courses to get my degree in business administration at the University of Applied Sciences in Friedberg, Germany. During the day I am a sales manager in a production facility.

For my bachelors thesis, I am performing a comprehensive statistical analysis of repair costs at the facility that I work.

After searching for days on Google for the right framework to solve this problem, I finally found the solution. The Excel Statistical Master has allowed me to find exactly the right distributions and showed me how to create some excellent graphs. The explanations and videos in the manual are excellent, even for a non-native English speaker!

Thanks Mark!"

Frank A. Mathias
Facility Management Major
Bachelor of Business Administration
University of Applied Sciences
Friedberg, Germany

"Whenever I evaluate a book on statistics, I always look at the table of contents to check both the topics covered and the examples.

Not only does the author cover all of the techniques you're likely to need in a graduate program, he also goes into substantial detail on when to use each technique.

I also found that his case studies and focused examples, all of which are listed in the detailed table of contents, were on point and good learning tools that will help learners know when and how to apply the techniques.

His explanations, particularly on when (and how) to use two-tailed tests for hypothesis testing and the Poisson and exponential distributions, were clear and will help anyone learn how to implement these techniques.

In particular, this book will help anyone without a substantial background in math, such as many political science M.A. students, to learn and apply the concepts.

Practical and Clear Graduate Statistics in Excel is very well done and well worth your money."

Curtis D. Frye
Author of
Microsoft Excel 2010 Plain & Simple

"I really like the Excel Statistical Master. It is incredibly useful. The explanations and videos in the manual are excellent.

It has really made my work with statistics a LOT easier. I'm really glad that I came across the manual.

If you're a student of business statistics, this e-manual is worth WAY more it's priced. I will use your manual as a reference for my Econometrics MBA course that I will be teaching this summer."

Dr. Yan Qin
Adjunct Assistant Professor of New York University
Adjunct Assistant Professor of Keller Graduate School of Management
Co-Director - Nankai-Grossman Center for Health Economics and Medical Insurance
New York, New York

"Faced with a seemingly intractable spreadsheet assignment for my online Operational Research course at a UK university and very little time, my purchase of this book could not have come at a better time.

With clear steps to follow, mastering the Statistical 'matter' and being able to apply them with Microsoft Excel assisted a great deal and broke down the 'hard nuts' in my spreadsheet assignment quickly.

I recommend this book if you are afraid of 'statistics'. It'll definitely drive those fears far away."

Toyin Lamikanra
Online Masters Program in Operational Research
University of Strathclyde

"I bought the Excel Statistical Master to help me in my statistics class. I must say, it was unbelievably useful. Not only did I master statistics in Excel, but <u>the e-manual actually did a much better job of explaining statistics than my text book did.</u>

That e-manual made my statistics class much easier to understand, and I am now able to do all of that stuff in Excel, easily ! It is a GREAT book ! <u>If you're a student or business manager wanting to learn statistics, this is easiest, fastest way to do it.</u>

Thank you again for everything."

Tiran Ovsepyan
North Hollywood, CA

"At first I was quite skeptical of this book and the attendant Microsoft Excel spreadsheets. Everyone touts how easy their product is and how you really "need" their product to be successful.

<u>For one of the few times I can remember, that claim is fulfilled with this product.</u>

I have been using Excel since the product first came out on the Macintosh. But the Excel Master series has shown me how really limited my knowledge was and how much there is yet to learn.

The Excel Master series is certainly an enjoyable and well constructed method of learning statistics. <u>The quality of the author's effort to reduce a relatively boring subject to easily understood examples and text is evident throughout.</u>

I highly recommend this series to anyone interested in the application of statistics to everyday problems using to most powerful computer environment available."

John G. Black
Warriors Mark, Pennsylvania

"I'm a PhD consultant in the area of "user experience". I help companies make their web sites user friendly. When I conduct a usability test on a web site design, I need to determine if one design is better than another. So I need to conduct a t-test. At other times, I conduct focus groups that help my client determine which of, say, 10 product designs is better than the others. So I need to conduct non-parametric ANOVAs on their rating responses.

All this goes to say, I need to deal with data rapidly, and in a manner that I can send to my client. Does my client have any statistical software? No, they don't have SyStat or MiniTab or SPSS, or any other packaged stats program. However, my clients DO have Excel.

With Excel, they can open my spreadsheet and see the data. While they are looking at the data (and perhaps running their own descriptive statistics like means, etc.) they can also see my statistical analysis I conducted with the Excel Statistical Master. They can see my charts, too.

So, you can imagine the benefit this gives to my client. It's "one-stop shopping". Data, analysis, and charts all appear in one file. I like being able to send one file that works with Microsoft Office. My client has Microsoft Office. Now they have everything they wanted: stats, data, and charts."

John Sorflaten, PhD Certified Usability Analyst (CUA)
Certified Professional Ergonomist (CPE)
Sr. Usability Engineer www.saic.com
Columbia, Maryland

"I'm a Statistician with more than 25 years of field work, at the same time I'm probably the top MS Excel expert in the Middle East.

Excel now is a Universal tool and an absolute must for those wishing to understand practical Statistics and applying Statistics to a very large percentage of real life situations.

All of the above facts require a clear understanding of the statistical features and capabilities of Excel. What is needed is a guide that takes you to the point DIRECTLY.

<u>As an Instructor Mr. Harmon's excellent work saves me considerable time, and should help all students.</u> And as a quick and direct revision tool for those applying Statistics in Business, Insurance, Medical Decision making and many more situations.

I can tell You that this Masterpiece is Very Very Very useful and would save you considerable time if you teach, but <u>If you are a Student...Please Pray for the Author... This is a GIFT from GOD</u>.

Keep it Up please."

Abdul Basit AL-Mahmood
Senior Consultant
ExcelTech
Kingdom of Bahrain

"We just started building statistical Excel spreadsheets for our direct mail and online marketing campaigns, I purchased Excel Statistical Master to help fill in some of the blanks.

Little did I know, this book has everything I could ever want to know about business statistics. <u>Easy to follow and written so even a child could understand some of the most complex statistical theories.</u>

Thanks Mark!"

Brandon Congleton
Marketing Director
www.WorldPrinting.com
Clearwater, Florida

"The Excel Statistical Master is a real life saver in my forensic accounting practice. Until I found the package I was struggling with some of the "how to" aspects of statistics..no more. The videos are an extra bonus that really help!

I am very pleased!!!"

Glenn Forrest
Seattle, WA

"As an engineering major in college, I never took statistics.

Now that I am a practicing engineer, statistics is an important part of my job - from reviewing test data to designing experiments and performing ANOVA.

The Excel Statistical Master series has helped me get up to speed faster than any traditional textbook.

I also found that my technical reports are more polished and professional as a result of my study of this material. The lessons are organized into logical groupings of topics and are just the right size for self-study or if you are using it as a course supplement.

Once I had mastered some of the basic topics I was able to skip around and study those topics I needed for my work. The ability to follow along with the exercises in Excel and then test out new scenarios is a real bonus and a great way to gain a feel for some of the concepts.

Since most of my work is done with Excel anyway, the exercises have served as templates for my job.

I highly recommend this series to anyone who works with statistics and also to the professional who desires to have a nicely organized reference for performing statistical calculations in Excel."

Chris Bronnenberg
Los Angeles, California

"Mark, I am quite impressed with the Excel Statistical Master.

As a research practitioner, I've used the easy-to-understand document to help work through some pretty daunting data sets.

As a professor of research, I will suggest the eManual as a supplement to my students.

I think the strength of the eManual is the straightforward explanations of complex procedures in a software platform that is readily available. SPSS and SAS should shudder at the competition.

Great job!"

Tait J. Martin, Ph.D.
President and Chief Insight Officer
The iNSiGHT Cooperative
Tallahassee, Florida

"The Excel Statistical Master eManual is a wonderful product for anyone who needs to apply a variety of statistical tools and does not have the time or background to develop those tools themselves.

The Excel Statistical Master is easy to use, comprehensive, and powerful.

Congratulations on an excellent product!"

Cliff Sather
Bennington, New England

"Going through Excel Statistical Master has helped me in filling the gaps which most of the professional ignore while building models from scratch.

There are many books in market available in market but the <u>Excel Statistical Master explains everything in a simple way</u> and how to use Excel to solve real life problems. <u>Every topic in Excel Statistical Master is self explanatory</u> and I would recommend freshmen as well as professionals to go through Excel Statistical Master.

Thanks Mark."

Ashutosh Gupta
Sr. Financial Analyst/Team Lead Mortgage Industry Advisory Corporation
Bengaluru, India

"My first encounter with the EXCEL Statistical Master came when writing a report for a customer when the axiom "an un-used tool becomes rusty" presented itself. I knew what analysis and presentation tool I wanted, but using EXCEL became cumbersome and frustrating.

A quick on-line check revealed <u>the EXCEL Statistical Master which proved to be unequivocal, easy to follow, and complete.</u>

Only after completing the report did I notice <u>the description on the front page "Clear And Simple yet Thorough."</u> Clearly, my experience supported substantiated this claim. <u>Seldom does one encounter such truth in advertising.</u>

Last weekend the manual was very useful in helping my grandson, who just started a statistics class in high school, help understand, envision, and define his semester project as to which data to gather and how to analyze and present that data.

I have recommended the Excel Statistical Master to customers and my contractors."

Pat Goodman
SSL Consulting
Morgan Hill, California

"I am an IT Consultant who gives a Data Analysis for Decision Making workshop to various private and public sector organizations. This workshop consists of many statistical methods.

I often use the Excel Statistical Master in my workshop to demonstrate procedures, give usable examples and frequently, learn new procedures myself.

I find it easy to use, clear and succinct. It should wipe out the fear of statistics from those who have a block against it."

Akram Najjar
Director
InfoConsult
IT Consulting
Beirut, Lebanon

If You Wish To Purchase It, Go To:

http://www.amazon.com/dp/B004SUR6H8

To Download the 2010 Excel Workbook

Containing All Examples In This Manual

Go to

http://excelmasterseries.com/D-_Loads/New____Examples.xlsx

CPSIA information can be obtained
at www.ICGtesting.com
Printed in the USA
LVHW061404260619
622426LV00028B/383/P